The part played by Royal Air Force Coastal Command during World War 2 has long been overshadowed by the more glamorous exploits of Fighter Command and by the controversial and hugely costly campaign waged by Bomber Command. Coastal Command is now best remembered for its pivotal role during the Battle of the Atlantic, the campaign upon which Britain's very survival — and the success of all later campaigns — ultimately depended. Though starved of resources for much of the time, Coastal Command fought a war arguably more important than the strategic bomber offensive, which dominated — and still dominates — the debate over Allied air strategy. By helping to preserve Britain's Atlantic lifeline to Canada and the United States and contributing decisively to the defeat of Hitler's U-boats, Coastal Command not only kept Britain in the war but also safeguarded the Allied build-up for the Second Front, thus ensuring final victory in Europe.

Important too was Coastal Command's anti-shipping campaign, directed with increasing power and accuracy against merchant vessels carrying strategically vital raw materials for use by German industry. Ranging along the enemy coast from the ports of western France to the fjords of northern Norway, Coastal Command's initially feeble offensive capabilities were transformed as the war progressed, culminating in the devastating Beaufighter and Mosquito strike wings that established a virtual blockade on economic traffic in the last months of the conflict. The effect on Hitler's armament programmes should not be understated, but this was another achievement overshadowed by the loud claims of the heavy bomber force.

Coastal Command began the war as nothing more than a small reconnaissance force, equipped with mostly unsuitable aircraft and lacking effective weapons or the means to deliver them. Its focus was the North Sea, where the Admiralty expected the naval war would be fought, and its principal task was to track the movement of Germany's major warships. It soon became apparent, however, that the main threat to the mercantile fleets on which Britain depended came not from battleships but U-boats, against which Coastal Command was at first virtually powerless. But with the supply of new aircraft, including many from the United States, and the development of improved tactics and weaponry, the situation gradually improved. Co-operating closely with the Royal Navy, Coastal Command drove the U-boats away from Britain's shores and reduced the areas of ocean in which they could safely operate. The anti-submarine squadrons were instrumental in gaining the upper hand in the Battle of the Atlantic and later contributed successfully to the invasion of Europe. The strike wings achieved a similar dominance over naval and mercantile vessels in coastal waters. By the end of the war Coastal Command had grown from a threadbare 'scarecrow' into a mighty weapon whose reach extended along the fringes of Europe and far out over the oceans.

This astonishing trans for this book, in which I have drawn together photographs from the Imperial War Museum's Photograph Archive. I have concentrated on the 'fighting arms' of Coastal Command, the front-line squadrons engaged in maritime reconnaissance and anti-shipping duties. Most were based in the United Kingdom, but I have also covered those units operating from such strategically vital locations as Iceland, Gibraltar and the Azores, which form an important part of the story. For much of the war Coastal Command was also responsible for administering the RAF's photo-reconnaissance units, but since these were employed largely in support of the strategic bombing effort over Europe I have not covered them here. Similarly the meteorological flights and a major part of the highly effective air-sea rescue service came under Coastal Command control in 1941. I have made only passing reference to their valuable work, which in truth deserves a book of its own.

Most of the photographs in the book were taken by members of the Royal Air Force Photographic Unit or shot unofficially by other service personnel. On occasions photographers were taken on operational sorties, but in most cases aircraft interior and air-to-air shots were set up for the cameras safely back at base. Fortunately, attacks on U-boats and enemy shipping were extensively recorded by the squadrons themselves, using aircraft-mounted and hand-held cameras, and many of these striking images are held in the IWM archives. The photograph captions are based on original information contained in Air Ministry files, supplemented by reference to various official records and published works. In recent years a great deal of new information has been unearthed concerning the fate of individual U-boats, and I have made use of this wherever possible to corroborate and in some cases correct established printed sources.

The quotations at the head of each chapter come from *Birds and Fishes — The Story of Coastal Command*, by Air Chief Marshal Sir Philip Joubert de la Ferté (published by Hutchinson & Co in 1960). This book provides a uniquely colourful and lively account of the development of Coastal Command and its subsequent wartime role, from the perspective of someone who for a time was in overall command. The principal secondary sources consulted are listed in the bibliography, and I am indebted to the authors of these works. I should also like to thank aviation historian Jerry Scutts for his assistance and interest in this project. Once again I owe a particular debt of gratitude to my wife Marian for proof-reading the manuscript. All the photographs are reproduced with the permission of the Imperial War Museum, and copies are available on application to the Photograph Archive.

Coastal Command lost a total of 10,875 personnel during World War 2. Although many crews completed one or more tours of operations without sighting the enemy, others were plunged

Above:
A Sunderland of No 210 Squadron watches over a troop convoy on its way to Britain, 31 July 1940: **CH 832**

into the thick of the action. Anti-shipping strikes were particularly hazardous, as were attacks on U-boats that chose to fight it out on the surface. At various times Luftwaffe fighters posed a serious threat, especially as most Coastal Command aircraft operated alone. Whatever the actions of the enemy, the weather and the sea itself were constant — and often greater — foes. In such hostile environments as the North Atlantic and the Arctic Ocean mechanical failure or navigational error could have disastrous consequences. Many crews sent on long patrols simply disappeared without trace. But no effort was spared to bring 'ditched' crews home, and some of the greatest individual acts of bravery and self-sacrifice were performed during rescue operations. I hope that in some way the courage, fortitude and indomitable spirit of the Coastal Command crews and the vital contribution of all those on the ground (and the water!) supporting them are conveyed through the photographs in this book.

INTRODUCTION

*'I wonder if Lord Trenchard and his successors in
the post of Chief of the Air Staff were not over-
inclined to concentrate on the bomber force for the
offensive, and on fighters for local defence. In
addition, of course, there would have been pressure
from the Army for close co-operation. These
influences shaped the pattern of the Royal Air
Force, and Coastal Command was an "also ran".'*

**(Air Chief Marshal Sir Philip Joubert de la Ferté,
Birds and Fishes — The Story of Coastal Command)**

The RAF's maritime role went back to World War 1, when coastal squadrons of the Royal Naval Air Service performed useful anti-submarine work, spotting for convoy escorts and harassing U-boats in the North Sea. In April 1918 a unified Royal Air Force was created when the RNAS was amalgamated with the Royal Flying Corps. By this time many air stations had been established around the coast of Britain, and the value of aircraft in protecting seaborne trade had been well demonstrated. Though lacking the weaponry to do any real damage to enemy U-boats (only one is believed to have actually been sunk by an aircraft acting alone), the effectiveness of the coastal squadrons as a 'scarecrow' force was certainly appreciated by the Royal Navy. Sadly this potential was not to be developed in the austere years that followed.

Instead, with the 'war to end all wars' over, the RAF in particular suffered huge cutbacks in its strength and underwent a major re-organisation. By the end of 1919 three separate geographic commands or 'Areas' — Northern, Southern and Coastal — had been formed. Coastal Area was responsible for what was left of the RAF's coastal squadrons, as well as the contingents of fleet-spotters and reconnaissance aircraft assigned to Royal Navy ships (the nucleus of the Fleet Air Arm). In 1920 Northern and Southern Areas merged to form a single Inland Area. By 1924 Coastal Area had only 29 operational aircraft, all of which were flying boats.

In this period of disarmament and economic retrenchment the RAF's very existence was safeguarded by the first Chief of the Air Staff, Sir Hugh Trenchard, who alerted the politicians to his Service's cost-effective potential in colonial policing operations. Trenchard effectively nurtured the RAF in its early days, but he was soon converted to the idea of creating a huge bomber force powerful enough to force a decision in any future conflict. The massed-bombing theories expounded by Trenchard and others dominated RAF strategic thinking in the two decades after World War 1, to the detriment of peripheral arms such as Coastal Area, which languished while the Admiralty and the new Air Staff bickered over its role.

The Admiralty expended a great deal of effort during the inter-war years trying to wrest back control of the Fleet Air Arm from the RAF, while losing its grip on the potential benefits of land-based maritime air power. It chose to believe that destroyers fitted with sound-location equipment (ASDIC) and the use of convoying procedures had been in themselves sufficient to ward off the U-boat threat in the previous war — and would be again in any future conflict. Meanwhile the Air Staff, distracted by the bomber theorists, paid scant attention to Coastal Area and chose to employ its squadrons in an imperial cruising role. In this new capacity the stately silver-painted flying boats reigned supreme, flying the flag in the far-flung corners of the Empire. Such exotic journeys may have had some political and diplomatic value but were scarcely relevant to the real objectives of maritime defence. Similarly, virtually nothing was done to create a coastal strike force suitable for attacking enemy shipping, save for equipping one squadron in 1928 with Hawker Horsley torpedo-bombers (an aircraft ordered simply to keep the company from folding!). The Air Staff saw little need for specialist aircraft when the strategic bomber force itself could be deployed against maritime targets, and at a longer range.

And so, despite a wealth of experience gained during World War 1, little was done during the inter-war years to further the potential of the RAF in the maritime environment. The lack of consideration paid to anti-submarine warfare was perhaps the most serious deficiency among many in these wasted years, and one that would have profound consequences at the beginning of World War 2. The long-range flying boats quartering the globe on their flag-waving missions were in many respects splendid aircraft but lacked any real offensive potential in this regard. The naval depth charge had been shown to be the most effective anti-U-boat weapon, but no attempt was made to devise an airborne version. Similarly, the few torpedo-bombers in service at the start of the 1930s were ill-suited to their task and represented nothing more than a token 'strike' force. Despite news of encouraging dive-bombing and torpedo trials in the USA, the RAF showed little enthusiasm for such specialised aircraft, being content to allow Coastal Area to stagnate while it concentrated on its all-consuming bomber doctrine. Likewise the Admiralty, though seeing some merit in coastal squadrons performing in a reconnaissance role, was equally obsessed with its own plans to rescue naval aviation from the RAF and restore maritime air power to its rightful place on the carrier flight-deck.

None of this would have mattered had not the rise of Nazism in Germany and militarism in Japan propelled the world towards a new conflict. Once the British Government had woken up to the threat from Hitler in the mid-1930s a massive rearmament programme was initiated. For the RAF a series of overlapping expansion schemes was set in motion, intended to rebuild its power and restore numerical parity with the new Luftwaffe. New

Above: A Vickers Vildebeest I, K2816, on display at King George V's Jubilee Review at Mildenhall in July 1935. The Vildebeest was the RAF's standard torpedo-bomber at this time, but only No 22 Squadron at Donibristle in Scotland was available to Coastal Command on its formation. In December 1936 a second squadron, No 42, was formed. For want of a modern replacement, both units continued to operate their obsolete aircraft until some months after the outbreak of war. **HU 3676**

Above: The Short Rangoon, a military version of the civilian Calcutta used by Imperial Airways, was the most antiquated of the flying boats in use with Coastal Command at its inception. The six that were completed all served with Nos 203 and 210 Squadrons before being phased out of service in the summer of 1936. **MH 2985**

Above: The Supermarine Scapa entered RAF service in 1935 as a successor to the long-serving Southampton. It was one of four different types of biplane flying boats in service with Coastal Command in 1936. Only 14 Scapas were built, serving mainly with Nos 202 and 204 Squadrons. By the end of 1938 all had been replaced by Saro Londons and Short Singapores. **MH 2994**

aircraft designs were ordered, new airfields constructed and airframe and aero-engine manufacturing output expanded. To cope with this enlargement the old administration was swept away, and in 1936 the RAF was organised into four functional commands — Bomber, Fighter, Coastal and Training. Not surprisingly, Coastal Command was the weakest, comprising only eight operational squadrons. It still retained responsibility for carrier and ship-board aviation, but in the following year the Fleet Air Arm was finally returned to Royal Navy control.

During the years of expansion Coastal Command's needs came a poor third to the other front-line commands. Not only was enlargement limited, but new strategic priorities and economic limitations also forced a re-think on the types of aircraft that should be ordered. In particular, concern was mounting that the large flying boats were generally unsuited to a war against Germany within the confines of the North Sea. The flying-boat lobby had held sway for almost two decades, but there now began something of a shift towards shorter-range land-planes, of which the first was the Avro Anson, ordered in 1934 for 'general reconnaissance' duties (as maritime reconnaissance was then known). The Anson's capabilities were

limited, but it was cheap enough to produce in large numbers at a time when numbers were paramount. By the end of 1936 two existing and two new squadrons in Coastal Command had been equipped with Ansons, and in the following year three more were formed.

Nevertheless, flying boats continued to play an important role, since the Admiralty —and many in the RAF also — believed strongly that only they were capable of long-range over-water operations. In 1936 Coastal Command had four flying boat squadrons, all operating different types — No 201 (Saro Londons), No 204 (Supermarine Scapas), No 209 (Short Singapores) and No 210 (Short Rangoons). The development of new aircraft continued, dominated by Supermarine, whose Scapa evolved into the Stranraer, and Shorts, whose more modern and vastly more capable four-engined Sunderland

Above: This Saro (Saunders-Roe) London, K5911, was delivered to No 204 Squadron at Mount Batten, Plymouth, in April 1937. Introduced into squadron service in the spring of 1936, Londons were still in use with three Coastal Command squadrons when war broke out. On 4 June 1941 this particular aircraft flew the RAF's last operational London patrol while on strength with No 202 Squadron at Gibraltar. **H(AM) 254**

entered service in 1938. However, an unfortunate consequence of the RAF's long-standing obsession with flying boats was that no long-range land-plane project was started, unlike in the USA, where the Boeing B-17 was designed to bomb enemy ships from high altitude, far out to sea. Such an aircraft would have solved many of Coastal Command's problems had it been available at the beginning of the war.

Some procurement decisions proved little short of a disaster for Coastal Command. In 1935 Air Ministry specifications were issued for aircraft to replace the Anson (never regarded as a serious front-line aircraft) and the obsolete Vickers Vildebeest, which by the end of 1936 equipped two torpedo-bomber squadrons. Because the Bristol Aeroplane Co was busy mass-producing Blenheim light bombers, the contract for a torpedo-capable general-reconnaissance aircraft was awarded to Blackburn, despite grave doubts being raised about the firm's management abilities and financial position. This decision to award a vital contract to Blackburn simply because it had spare manufacturing capacity proved a huge mistake, as the aircraft it came up with — the Botha — was both slow in its gestation and irredeemably flawed. Bristol's own more promising design, the Beaufort, was accepted for a parallel torpedo-bombing requirement, but the project was hamstrung by the priority being

given to the Blenheim programme and by time wasted on an interim design based on the Blenheim, called the Bolingbroke. By early 1938, with these new aircraft either failing or delayed, the Air Ministry was forced to look abroad for existing aircraft to fill the gap.

The British Purchasing Mission sent to the United States in March 1938 ordered 200 Lockheed Hudsons for Coastal Command, of which the first would arrive in early 1939. Derived from a civilian airliner, the Hudson was a sound design capable of carrying a reasonable bomb load, and with enough endurance to operate across the North Sea. The decision was a fortuitous one, because by November 1938 the Bolingbroke project was dead in the water, and the Chief of the Air Staff was calling — unsuccessfully — for the Botha to be scrapped as well. The Beaufort, meanwhile, was still over a year away from entering squadron service. As a result Coastal Command would

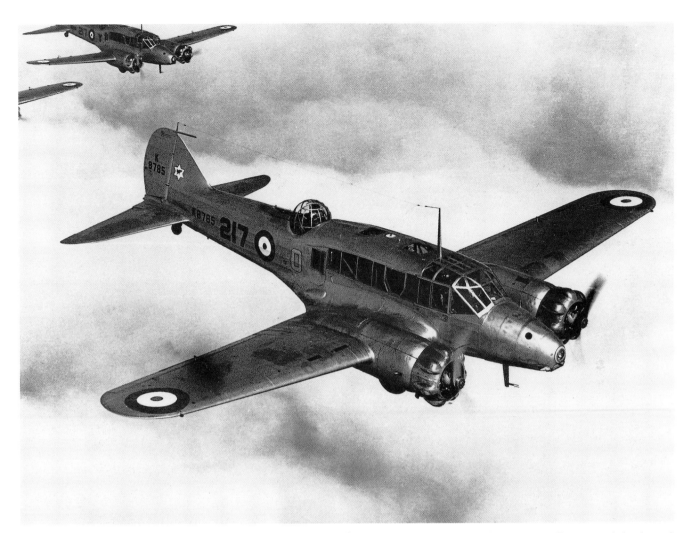

be forced to enter World War 2 with the Anson as its main general-reconnaissance type and with two squadrons of antiquated Vildebeests as its sole strike component.

A similar *débâcle* surrounded the 1936 procurement of a modern short-range flying boat. The Air Ministry gave the contract to Saunders-Roe (Saro), another company with a suspect management record but the only one with spare manufacturing capacity. By early 1939 the Lerwick was nowhere near operational service, and its inadequate performance giving cause for concern. Meanwhile one of the US Navy's Consolidated PBY flying boats was ordered for testing, but only 30 of these outstanding 'maritime patrol bombers' were initially ordered. Once again, the decision to persevere with an unsuitable aircraft such as the Lerwick merely delayed the procurement of a tried and tested design from the USA. It was a disastrous policy for the RAF, especially in view of the fact that the completion of sound home-grown aircraft such as the Beaufort and the Sunderland was hindered by the priority given to bomber and fighter production. The failure of the Lerwick meant that Coastal Command went to war with obsolete London and Stranraer flying boats still in operational service.

One successful outcome of this period was a reorganisation of the command structure of Coastal Command. Its three main group headquarters and their areas of control were aligned with those of existing naval HQs. These new Area Combined HQs, with joint operations rooms staffed by RAF and naval officers, simplified the chain of command and facilitated close liaison. By the summer of 1939 No 15 Group headquarters was at Plymouth, No 16 Group was located at Chatham, and No 18 Group was at Donibristle, near Rosyth. A fourth, No 17 Group, was dedicated to training and centred on Gosport. Coastal Command headquarters itself was moved from Lee-on-Solent to Northwood, near London, to be closer to the Admiralty and the corridors of power.

In September 1939 Coastal Command fielded 19 operational squadrons. Ten were equipped with Ansons, two of them in the process of converting to Hudsons; another squadron was already fully equipped with Hudsons, and there were two squadrons of Vildebeest torpedo-bombers. The flying-boat contingent comprised three squadrons of Sunderlands, two of Londons and one of Stranraers. In overall command was Air Marshal (soon to be Air Chief Marshal) Sir Frederick Bowhill, a former RNAS aviator well versed in naval matters. He controlled fewer than 200 available aircraft, most of which were obsolescent and suitable only for short-range operations. Of this 'hotch-potch' only the Sunderlands and the small number of Hudsons then in service could be characterised as modern. There were no effective bombs or other anti-submarine weapons, and many crews were not fully trained. But Coastal Command was not expected to play a decisive role in the new war — its principal task was to be one of reconnaissance and fleet support, with the defence of seaborne trade only a subsidiary function. Bowhill, though, had long suspected that enemy submarines would pose a bigger threat than the Admiralty supposed. He was right, and his Command was nowhere near ready to face it.

Below: Short Singapore III K8856 moored at Mount Batten in May 1937. This aircraft was one of the last of the stately Singapores to be built and was delivered initially to No 228 Squadron. After operational service it was retired to the FBTS (Flying Boat Training Squadron) at Calshot, near Southampton, in whose hands it was written off in December 1939. **H(AM) 273**

Right: Enter the Sunderland. Of all the aircraft used by Coastal Command, the Short Sunderland, which entered service in June 1938, is perhaps the most famous. This is the prototype, K4774, on the slipway at Short's plant at Rochester, soon after roll-out in October 1937. The vast aircraft, developed in parallel with the civilian C-class 'Empire' flying boat, was an advanced all-metal, stressed-skin design. Spacious and well-equipped, it was a world away from the biplane 'boats then in service with the RAF. Like the Anson, the Sunderland was to enjoy an extended and very successful service life. **ATP 9278C**

Below right: Another new-generation flying boat, designed to serve alongside the Sunderland, was the Saro Lerwick. L7248 was the first to be built, and is seen here at the MAEE (Marine Aeroplane Experimental Establishment) at Felixstowe in the autumn of 1938. Though very modern in construction and appearance, the Lerwick's flight dynamics were fundamentally flawed, and tests revealed it to be very unstable in the air and on the water. **MH 3048**

Above: Supermarine Stranraer K7297 of No 228 Squadron cutting a majestic wake on its take-off run at Pembroke Dock, in South Wales, late 1938. Other aircraft, some camouflaged, are moored in the background. The Stranraer was the last of the biplane flying boats to enter Coastal Command service, the first production aircraft going to No 228 Squadron in April 1937. K7297 went missing in bad weather over the North Sea in August 1939 while serving with No 209 Squadron.
HU 67366

Above: The Blackburn Botha was another product of the RAF's expansion and re-equipment programme in the late 1930s and was designed to replace the Anson and the Vildebeest in the general-reconnaissance and torpedo-bombing roles. Like the Lerwick, the Botha was unwisely ordered directly off the drawing board, without a prototype stage, and failed to live up to expectations. The first was L6104, seen here, which took to the air in December 1938, but examples were not delivered to the RAF until the summer of 1940. **MH 5171**

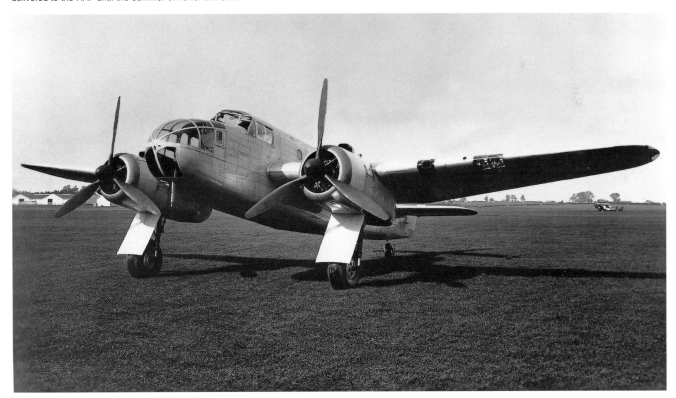

Above: The final new aircraft built for Coastal Command during the last years of peace was the Bristol Beaufort torpedo-bomber. Original plans, later revised, were for it to equip overseas squadrons only, as the Botha was intended for home-based units. The first aircraft completed was L4441, seen here at the time of its maiden flight in October 1938. The large forward-opening wheel-well doors caused instability on approach and were quickly discarded. Less easily fixed were numerous problems with its Taurus engines, which significantly delayed its entry into service. **MH 3178**

1939

'There was no glamour, no offensive attitude, attached to the aircraft whose duty was, under God and the Royal Navy, to assure the essential supplies to an island fortress. But Coastal possessed one very great asset, the spirit of its personnel.'

(Air Chief Marshal Sir Philip Joubert de la Ferté, *Birds and Fishes — The Story of Coastal Command*)

On 3 September 1939 Prime Minister Neville Chamberlain mournfully informed the people of Britain that, following Hitler's refusal to withdraw his forces from Poland, a state of war now existed with Germany. The authorities waited anxiously for a mass bombing assault from the air. Civil defence measures were in place and hospital wards prepared — but nothing happened. What was soon to be dubbed the 'Phoney War' — a period of nervous anticipation and bemused anti-climax — had begun. It was a different story at sea, however, where the war was anything but 'phoney' for the men of the Royal and Merchant Navies. Coastal Command too was called into action from the very start, its slender resources employed on two main tasks. The first — and, as far as the Admiralty was concerned, the most important — was to locate enemy warships in the North Sea. The second was to shepherd the many British and Allied merchant ships that now found themselves exposed to attack as they made course for British ports.

For years the Royal Navy had been confident of its ability to deal with U-boats, using destroyers fitted with sound-location equipment (ASDIC), and believed that German commerce raiders, especially the so-called 'pocket battleships', represented the greater threat if they managed to break out of the North Sea into the Atlantic shipping lanes. These convictions coincided with directives already issued concerning the offensive role of the RAF in time of war. Bomber Command, forbidden to bomb German territory for fear of injuring civilians (or damaging private property!), was ordered instead to seek out German warships at sea. Coastal Command was to share the task of reconnaissance, covering the area between Scotland and the Norwegian coast, even if its aircraft lacked the means to interfere with the passage of any such vessels discovered.

However, events quickly overturned established priorities. The sinking of the passenger liner *Athenia* by *U-30* on the first day of the war gave tragic notice of the real peril to seaborne trade and communications. The Admiralty, suddenly alarmed at the prospect of unrestricted submarine warfare, ordered convoying to begin immediately. But with many of its U-boats already on station and with a large number of Allied merchant vessels sailing without protection, the Kriegsmarine reaped a bumper harvest during the first month of the war. Of a total of 53 ships sunk in September, U-boats accounted for no fewer than 41.

As a consequence Coastal Command was directed to give equal weight to reconnaissance and anti-submarine activities.

The North Sea reconnaissance patrols were continued into the winter months. They were flown in the main by the Anson squadrons of No 18 Group, but their aircraft lacked sufficient range to completely cover the designated area of operations and were forced to turn back at least 50 miles short of the coast of southern Norway. Royal Navy submarines were employed to cover the gap. The longer-range Hudsons of No 224 Squadron, based at Leuchars, and the ageing London and Stranraer flying boats, operating from Sullom Voe and Invergordon, were also employed as part of the search force. On 8 October a No 224 Squadron Hudson sighted the battlecruiser *Gneisenau* with a strong escort heading towards Norway. The Home Fleet and other Royal Navy units came out to intercept, without success, and attacks by Bomber Command Wellingtons also failed. The weather, often atrocious in the North Sea, was a recurrent problem, as was the time that elapsed between sighting potential targets and the arrival of naval and air strike forces. Consequently the German surface fleet, never keen to confront the Royal Navy, remained extremely elusive. In November the 'pocket battleship' *Deutschland* slipped back from its Atlantic patrol without interference. Later that month the *Gneisenau* and *Scharnhorst* made a sortie out to the Faeroes–Iceland passage, where they sank the auxiliary cruiser *Rawalpindi*, before evading strong British naval forces in bad weather and reaching port, again without being detected.

During this period there were numerous engagements over the North Sea between Coastal Command aircraft and Luftwaffe reconnaissance machines. The first air-to-air combat occurred on 5 September, when an Anson of No 206 Squadron was shot down by a pair of Heinkel He115 seaplanes off the Frisian Islands. The pilot, Pilot Officer L. H. Edwards, was the only survivor and was picked up by one of the Heinkels. On 8 October a 'battle flight' of three Hudsons from No 224 Squadron came across a Dornier Do18 flying boat. The Hudsons attacked, forcing the Dornier to alight on the sea, where it was abandoned by its crew. It was the first victory of the war by RAF aircraft based in Britain. In November No 220 Squadron, which had recently begun converting to Hudsons, fought four separate engagements, claiming two Do18s without loss. An unusual combat took place east of the Shetlands on 19 December between a London flying boat of No 240 Squadron and a Heinkel He111. Both aircraft limped away after suffering damage. In the case of the London the captain was mortally wounded, and his aircraft written off after the co-pilot flew it back to Sullom Voe.

Now that the magnitude of the U-boat threat had been revealed, Coastal Command found itself stretched to the limit. Areas it had to cover included the Channel, the East Coast

*Above:*The Avro Anson was by far the most numerous type in Coastal Command service at the beginning of the war, equipping 10 squadrons in the general-reconnaissance role. Though stable and dependable, it was let down by a very limited range (radius of action was approximately 250 nautical miles) and an utterly inadequate bomb-load (a pair of 100lb bombs were usually carried for anti-submarine patrol work). These aircraft of No 220 Squadron are flying in formation for the benefit of the camera; operational patrols were normally flown alone. **HU 91217**

convoy route between the Firth of Forth and the Thames Estuary, the Bristol Channel and the Irish Sea. Patrols were also flown along the North Sea coastline of the Low Countries. It was off the Dutch coast on 5 September that a No 206 Squadron Anson, commanded by Pilot Officer R. T. Kean, attacked a U-boat from low level. The Anson was damaged from the explosion of its own bombs and forced to return to base. It was a nerve-racking time for the young New Zealand pilot — four days later he was forced to ditch in the Channel after running out of fuel! On 8 November Ansons from the same squadron shot an He115 into the sea off the Frisian island of Texel and damaged another. Such were the demands on Coastal Command's resources that even the crews of Nos 22 and 42 Squadrons flew reconnaissance patrols in their ancient Vickers Vildebeest torpedo bombers.

Meanwhile the Sunderlands of Nos 204, 210 and 228 Squadrons ranged westwards into the Atlantic, flying convoy escorts and anti-submarine patrols over the North- and South-Western Approaches. The flying boats carried out several attacks on U-boats, but no confirmed kills were reported. Unfortunately the Sunderlands, which alone among Coastal Command aircraft possessed the range to remain on station for extended periods, could not be everywhere at once, prompting the Admiralty to resort to extreme measures. Three aircraft

carriers were diverted to anti-submarine duties, using their own embarked aircraft to fill gaps in the air cover. The experiment proved a disaster. On 17 September HMS *Courageous* was torpedoed and sunk southwest of Ireland, with great loss of life. HMS *Ark Royal* narrowly avoided a similar fate.

For inshore protection Coastal Command formed six coastal patrol flights, based at various stations around the country. Equipped only with Tiger or Hornet Moth biplanes and usually operating in pairs, these 'scarecrow patrols' operated low over the approaches to major inlets and harbours. Their task, as the name suggests, was to 'spook' any U-boats into diving, their only weapons flare pistols with which to signal the presence of enemy submarines to nearby Royal Navy vessels. The patrols began in December and continued throughout the hard winter of 1939/40. The pilots, frozen and bored, invariably saw nothing. Another stop-gap measure was the temporary transfer of No 58 Squadron from Bomber

Command to Coastal at the end of September. The squadron's Whitley III bombers patrolled the western end of the English Channel, once again without incident.

Fortunately for the British, sinkings by U-boats fell sharply after their initial period of success in September. The rapid instigation of the convoy system (for ships sailing at 9-15 knots) was a major contributor to this, although the slowest and fastest ships, sailing independently, remained acutely vulnerable. A more significant factor was a reduction in U-boat numbers. The concentration of U-boats gathered in operational areas before the outbreak of war could not be maintained and shrank as many boats returned to port for repairs and re-supply. In fact the U-boat force itself was numerically extremely weak (fewer than 50 being available), and the number of boats on station in any one area of operations rarely exceeded half a dozen. This knowledge would have been of limited comfort to the Naval Staff, however, now drastically revising its appreciation of the U-boat threat in the light of recent events.

Another headache for the Royal Navy was the magnetic mine, now being dropped by the Germans into Britain's coastal waters. A priority programme was set up to counter this particular weapon, starting with the recovery and defusing (by Lieutenant Commander John Ouvry RN) of a mine exposed on mudflats at Shoeburyness, in the Thames Estuary. From this heroic deed were garnered the weapon's secrets, and an antidote found. Ships were 'degaussed' — their magnetic fields neutralised — by fitting

a cable around them, through which an electric current was passed. A stranger countermeasure came in the form of a Wellington bomber fitted with a giant ring-shaped electro-magnet. Given the deliberately misleading code-name of DWI (Directional Wireless Installation), the apparatus allowed the aircraft to explode mines by flying low over the water. Put under the administrative control of No 16 Group, Coastal Command, the first DWI Wellington was ready for operations in January 1940.

Nine enemy submarines were sunk between September and December 1939, but all were accounted for by mines or units of the Royal Navy. Attacks by Coastal Command aircraft had come to naught. The key factor in this disappointing start, apart from the obvious shortage of aircraft and trained crews, was the complete lack of an effective anti-submarine weapon. An infamous incident of mistaken identity on 3 December served only to reinforce the point that sighting surfaced submarines was not the main problem; having the means to destroy them was. A British submarine, HMS *Snapper*, suffered only blown light bulbs and smashed crockery after receiving a direct hit from a 100lb AS (Anti-Submarine) bomb. This weapon, and the larger 250-pounder, lacked a sufficient weight of explosive to be effective. What was needed was a 'thin-cased' weapon, with a reliable hydrostatic fuse to ensure it exploded underwater. Development of an airborne version of the Royal Navy's standard 450lb depth charge was given top priority.

New weapons and aircraft would also be needed for Coastal Command's war against surface shipping. For the present, Government policy restricted RAF attacks specifically to warships and troop transports. No offensive action was to be taken against merchantmen. In view of the fact that the Command's dedicated strike force comprised two squadrons of Vildebeests, such distinctions were largely academic. The first Bristol Beaufort torpedo-bombers had been delivered, but owing to various design flaws their entry into service was to be a protracted one. The adaptable Hudson was therefore pressed into the maritime strike role, and by the end of the year the type was in service with three squadrons. One of these, No 220, carried out the Command's first attack on an enemy warship, on 13 December. On 27 December another No 220 Squadron aircraft sighted a group of enemy destroyers and minesweepers and claimed a hit on the stern of one of them in a dive-bombing attack through a curtain of flak. The Hudson was far from suited to the task, but as was the case throughout Coastal Command — and, indeed, much of the RAF

in general at this time — it was a question of making do.

By the end of 1939 Coastal Command, through no lack of offensive spirit or courage, had failed to make its mark in any decisive way, especially against the U-boats. But despite obvious deficiencies it had quickly become 'U-boat-minded' and was settling into its mainstream role. Long anti-submarine patrols, with crews spending hour after monotonous hour gazing intently at a grey ocean, would constitute the Command's 'bread and butter' work for the rest of the war. And the lack of any definite kills up to this point ignored the less tangible (but nevertheless valuable) deterrent effect the aircraft were providing. The U-boats may well have claimed even more hapless victims had not at least some of their number been forced to dive and evade after spotting an aircraft — even a Tiger Moth — on the horizon. The RAF crews were accumulating valuable skills, not least the art of navigating over featureless expanses of ocean, often in marginal conditions. They had little to show for it, but they were learning.

Below: The SS *Kensington Court* sinking by the bow on 18 September 1939, as seen from one of three Sunderlands from No 228 Squadron involved in the rescue of her crew. The ship had been shelled by a surfaced U-boat 70 miles west of the Isles of Scilly. While one aircraft circled overhead to deter further U-boat attacks, two more alighted to pick up the survivors — no mean feat, as the Sunderland was never designed to land on the choppy waters of the open ocean. **C 2**

Opposite top: First of the 'Cats'. Consolidated Model 28-5 (PBY) patrol-bomber P9630, on test at the MAEE at Felixstowe in 1939. Such were the qualities of this American long-range maritime aircraft — and the inadequacies of home-grown products such as the Lerwick — that 60 had been ordered by the beginning of the war, and more were obtained by taking over French contracts. Named the Catalina by the RAF, the PBY would eventually enter service in March 1941 and would go on to become one of Coastal Command's most successful aircraft, with over 600 being delivered during the course of the war. **MH 3043**

Left: A group of Royal Australian Air Force pilots and ground staff had been sent to Britain to ferry an order of Sunderlands back to Australia, but on the outbreak of war they were retained for service in Britain instead. Loaned to the RAF for operational duties, they were attached temporarily to No 210 Squadron. Their commanding officer, Wing Commander Leon Lachal (left), is seen here with four of his captains at Pembroke Dock in December 1939 — (from left) Flight Lieutenant William 'Hoot' Gibson, Flight Lieutenant Charles Pearce, Pilot Officer Ivan Podger and Flight Lieutenant William 'Bill' Garing. The Australians would form the nucleus of a new squadron in Coastal Command, No 10 RAAF, officially declared operational in January 1940. **C 231**

Below: Two airmen demonstrate the dorsal armament of a Sunderland at Pembroke Dock, December 1939. The Sunderland I had a pair of .303in Vickers 'K' guns in this position, fired through hatches and protected from the slipstream by retractable fairings (shown retracted in this photograph). Later versions of the aircraft were fitted with a mid-upper turret. **C 243**

Opposite bottom: Australian engine fitters training on a Sunderland's starboard outer Bristol Pegasus XXII at Pembroke Dock. Standard ladders and trestles could not be used when working on flying boats moored on the water, so the Sunderland was fitted with specially-designed servicing platforms that retracted into the leading edge of the wing, seen in use here. **C 232**

Above: A pair of 250lb anti-submarine bombs suspended beneath the wing of a Saro London. Experience during World War 1 had shown that, to have any chance of destroying a U-boat, thin-cased, high-capacity depth charges had to be detonated below the surface. In the intervening years these hard-won lessons had been forgotten, and the three sizes of bomb available to Coastal Command at the beginning of the war were quite unsuited to the task. The standard 100lb device was virtually useless, and it was discovered that even the 500-pounder had to explode within 8ft of a submarine's hull to cause major damage. **HU 3171**

Right: A convoy in 'northern waters', seen from a No 240 Squadron Saro London, late 1939. Convoying had been quickly instituted after the sinking of the *Athenia* on the first day of the war, although many ships continued to sail independently. The first U-boat attack on a convoy took place on 16 September, when *U-31* stalked OB4, westbound from Liverpool. In the following months a thinly-spread Coastal Command did what it could to offer protection to vessels around Britain's shores, but its range was limited, and mercantile losses were heavy. **M 408**

> '*So began the thrust which pushed the U-boats away from our shores and out into the wide Atlantic. But Coastal was sadly short of long-range aircraft and our ships without air escort continued to be sunk...*'
>
> (Air Chief Marshal Sir Philip Joubert de la Ferté, *Birds and Fishes — The Story of Coastal Command*)

Coastal Command entered the first full year of the war in desperate need of new squadrons and aircraft. Unfortunately, two new types ordered as part of the Command's prewar re-equipment programme, the Saro Lerwick and Blackburn Botha, had turned out to be major disappointments and would play little part in events. The Lerwick commenced operations with No 209 Squadron in December 1939, but experience quickly revealed the aircraft's many flaws, and few were left after a dismal year of service. The Botha entered service with No 608 Squadron in August 1940, but it too would be hastily withdrawn from the front line. A third and ultimately more successful new design, the Bristol Beaufort, had been delivered to No 22 Squadron at Thorney Island. The squadron was working up on the new type over the winter, but because it was dogged by a number of technical problems the first operational sorties would not take place until April.

Coastal Command's general-reconnaissance squadrons were gradually replacing their Ansons — 'Faithful Annies' — with the more capable Hudson. No 224 Squadron had recently fitted some of its aircraft with ASV (Air-to-Surface Vessel) Mk I radar. Though unable to detect a surfaced submarine beyond two or three miles, in favourable conditions the radar could identify a larger target (such as a ship) up to 20 miles away, and it was a useful aid to navigation as well. The first recorded operational use of this primitive equipment occurred on 10 January, when No 224's battle flight, operating from Wick, used it to locate an enemy convoy. No 206 Squadron flew its first Hudson sortie on 12 April, a reconnaissance of the Frisian islands of Borkum and Texel. Four 'trade protection' squadrons were transferred from Fighter Command in February and began operations with Blenheim IVFs during the spring. Their initial task was fishery protection in the North Sea, but they later took on a variety of jobs including naval escort, fighter-reconnaissance and offensive sweeps. The Blenheim squadrons played an increasingly important part in Coastal Command operations during 1940, and five more were formed or transferred from other Commands before the year was out.

The Sunderlands continued their vital long-range convoy-escort activities, the usual practice being for a single aircraft to remain at close hand to the ships during daylight hours. At this time the convoys were relatively safe, as the U-boats preferred to pick on ships sailing alone. February was a peak month for sinkings, with 45 ships being sent to the bottom. On 30 January Coastal Command finally achieved a U-boat 'kill', albeit one shared with the Navy. A Sunderland of No 228 Squadron joined with several convoy escorts in an attack on *U-55* southwest of the Isles of Scilly. After a severe depth-charging the U-boat was abandoned and scuttled. The first clash between a Sunderland and the Luftwaffe occurred on 3 April 1940, when a No 204 Squadron aircraft on a convoy escort survived attacks by several Ju88s and shot down at least one of them during the action. By this time No 10 Squadron, Royal Australian Air Force, had become operational, and No 201 Squadron had also begun replacing its antiquated Londons with Sunderlands.

In February Coastal Command aircraft played a major role in locating the *Altmark*, formerly the supply ship to the 'pocket battleship' *Admiral Graf Spee* and now attempting to return to Germany. Air searches were instigated following intelligence tip-offs, and on 16 February a Hudson crew of No 220 Squadron discovered the ship sheltering in the 'neutral' waters of a Norwegian fjord. That night the destroyer HMS *Cossack* was ordered to enter the fjord and effect its capture, thereby releasing the crews of five merchant ships held aboard. The operation, personally ordered by Winston Churchill, First Lord of the Admiralty, was a huge propaganda coup for the British but finally persuaded Hitler that action would have to be taken against Norway to protect Germany's interests.

The British and French Governments had long been exerting pressure on both Norway and Sweden, claiming their continuing neutrality was harmful to the Allied cause. The prime concern was the export of Swedish iron ore to Germany. Over half the high-grade ore required by the German steel industry was imported from Sweden. Much of it was shipped via the ice-free port of Narvik in northern Norway (the alternative route from the Swedish port of Lulea, on the northern shore of the Baltic, being ice-bound during the winter). The convoys from Narvik, hugging the Norwegian coast, brought other essential raw materials, such as copper, nickel and fertilisers, to Germany, and the same ships took back coke, coal and other goods in return payment. Interrupting this traffic, as part of a wider economic blockade on Germany, was now regarded as a vital strategic objective.

After much prevarication the War Cabinet finally agreed to start laying mines in Norwegian waters and readied troops to invade. But the Germans, well aware of Allied moves and determined to forestall their plans, struck first. By 6 April an invasion force was at sea and heading for Norway. Despite intelligence warnings and the evidence from air reconnaissance the Admiralty preferred to believe the Germans were bluffing. Over the next 48 hours Coastal Command located major naval units in the North Sea, including the heavy cruiser *Admiral*

Hipper. During one such reconnaissance patrol on 8 April a Sunderland of No 204 Squadron was shot down by an He111 west of Bergen. The next day the Germans penetrated Norwegian territorial waters, occupying the capital, Oslo, and other key ports.

The campaign in Norway in April and May 1940 was the first major escalation of the war. In contrast to the Wehrmacht's meticulously planned operation, conducted under a blanket of air cover, the Allied military response was typically unco-ordinated and weakly supported. British troops landed at Namsos and Andalsnes in mid-April but were soon repulsed. A landing at Narvik at the end of May, though more successful, also resulted in an evacuation. The Royal Navy was demonstrably more effective, and in several actions wreaked havoc on the Kriegsmarine. As for the RAF, although Bomber Command played a part it fell to Coastal Command to bear the brunt of air operations. Its aircraft flew reconnaissance sorties and defensive patrols, supplementing the Navy's carrier-based fighters and dive-bombers. The Luftwaffe was a constant threat, and the lack of a suitable long-range fighter was keenly felt. The Blenheim IVFs of No 254 Squadron, based at Lossiemouth, were forced to plug the gap, but these aircraft were scarcely capable of tackling German fighters on equal terms. Sunderlands

too were heavily involved in the campaign, flying reconnaissance sorties, transporting stores and evacuating wounded.

In the anti-shipping war the gloves had come off at last, and Coastal Command's main effort was concentrated along the Norwegian coast. No 233 Squadron claimed the Command's first successful attack on an enemy ship, when the merchant vessel *Theodor* was damaged in Grimstad Fjord on 29 April. Restrictions governing which ships could be attacked had already been relaxed, and on 4 May the Air Ministry issued a formal notice sanctioning strikes on any vessel, whatever its type or flag, found within 10 miles of the Norwegian coast. The Hudson squadrons formed the backbone of Coastal Command's anti-shipping force but were far from ideal. Trained for the general-reconnaissance role, their crews now had to learn appropriate bombing techniques. A major problem was the lack of an effective bombsight. The Hudson's Mk IX sight was not accurate enough to hit a small target such as a single ship, and

Below: King George VI and Queen Elizabeth visited the Bristol Aeroplane Company at Filton, near Bristol, on 7 February 1940. They are seen here being shown one of the new Beauforts (probably L4442, the second to be completed) by Captain Cyril Unwins, Bristol's chief test pilot. Not yet operational, the Beaufort was undergoing vigorous service trials with No 22 Squadron at Thorney Island on the South Coast, where its unreliable engines were a major cause for concern. **C 667**

on low-level attacks the skipper usually resorted to bombing by eye, which meant just as the ship was passing below his aircraft! Navigation standards also required improvement. The simple parallel-line patrols over the North Sea had been abandoned in favour of more sophisticated 'crossover' and 'box' patrols and free-ranging armed reconnaissance sorties. In addition, patrols along Norway's southwest coastline brought the Hudsons within range of the Luftwaffe, and encounters with enemy fighters steadily increased during this period.

Meanwhile, the aircraft intended to replace the Vildebeest in the dedicated anti-shipping role — the Bristol Beaufort — was struggling with major engine problems. Fourteen Beauforts had been delivered to No 22 Squadron by April 1940. These aircraft were employed initially for mine-laying off the Dutch coast but after several crashes were grounded pending modifications to their Bristol Taurus engines. On 7 May six aircraft carried out the squadron's first offensive sortie, a bombing attack on a destroyer off the Frisians, but the ship escaped unscathed, and one Beaufort failed to return. No 42 Squadron received its first Beauforts in April, but again engine problems and other technical difficulties hindered early operations.

On 10 May attention was drawn away from Norway when the Germans invaded France and the Low Countries, precipitating a series of events that would end with France being knocked out of the war and the British Expeditionary Force (BEF) retreating to Dunkirk. Again, Coastal Command was heavily engaged, carrying out defensive patrols and bombing attacks, as well as ensuring that U-boats and other enemy naval craft were unable to interfere with the evacuation of the BEF. On 11 May Blenheims of No 235 Squadron covered the landing of British troops at The Hague — and their subsequent evacuation some days later. Beauforts of No 22 Squadron bombed Rotterdam airport, and struck at enemy torpedo boats at Ijmuiden. On 18 May three squadrons of Hudsons took part in night

bombing raids on oil-storage tanks in Hamburg and Bremen. With Operation 'Dynamo' underway, Hudsons and Ansons flew crossover patrols along the now occupied coast and above the Dunkirk beaches themselves. Coastal Command crews were not reluctant to engage enemy aircraft, even if the odds appeared hopeless; in one celebrated incident on 1 June an Anson of No 500 Squadron, flown by Pilot Officer Philip Peters, shot down two Me109s!

In early June the Norwegian campaign finally drew to a close, but Coastal Command was still active in the area, carrying out some major attacks on heavy German naval units. On 11 June 12 Hudsons of No 269 Squadron bombed the battlecruiser *Scharnhorst* and other ships in Trondheim harbour from 15,000ft. Hits were claimed on two vessels, but the *Scharnhorst* escaped damage and two Hudsons were lost to flak and fighters. Two days later Beauforts of No 22 Squadron carried out diversionary attacks on nearby Vaernes airfield, while Fleet Air Arm Skuas were decimated in another strike on the ship. On 21 June Hudsons took part in yet another attack on the *Scharnhorst*, this time near Bergen. No 233 Squadron's commanding officer, Squadron Leader Dunstan Feeny, and his crew were killed when their aircraft was attacked by fighters during the run-in and exploded in flames. Three No 42 Squadron Beauforts from a force of nine were also shot down by Me109s in a follow-up attack on the same day.

After the fall of France and Norway Britain found herself directly threatened by the victorious Wehrmacht. The occupation of western France and Norway also gave the

Above: Local lifeboatmen were invited to spend a day at RAF Leuchars, near Dundee, in March 1940, the highlight being a flight in a No 224 Squadron Hudson. Here the squadron CO, Wing Commander E. A. Hodgson, helps one of their number out of the aircraft after the trip. The bath-shaped door of the Hudson housed the inflatable dinghy and survival equipment. This aircraft, N7272, was lost on 20 November 1940, when it ran out of fuel and had to be abandoned by its crew, eventually crashing in Loch Lomond. **HU 91235**

Germans a vastly expanded base from which her U-boats and surface forces could prey on shipping in the Atlantic and North Sea. Coastal Command's range of activities was greatly increased as a consequence. Anti-invasion patrols in the English Channel became a priority, alongside a renewed anti-shipping effort. The results of the latter were meagre. Between June and September Coastal Command sank only two ships at sea, though a number of others were damaged. At least there could be little confusion over identifying suitable targets — practically anything afloat from the northern reaches of Norway to the frontier of Spain was now considered fair game. During that memorable summer, as the Battle of Britain was fought out over southern England, Coastal Command maintained its patrols and mine-laying activities and participated in attacks on the ports and harbours where Hitler's invasion forces were gathering. Two more Blenheim squadrons, Nos 53 and 59 from

Army Co-operation Command, were transferred to Coastal in July and flew reconnaissance patrols. Fairey Battle squadrons from Bomber Command were also temporarily attached and joined in the bombing raids on barge concentrations.

On 11 September the Beaufort was finally employed in its intended role. On that day five torpedo-armed aircraft of No 22 Squadron were sent to attack three merchantmen off Ostend. One ship was hit and damaged. On 17 September the squadron carried out a successful night attack on ships in Cherbourg harbour, sinking one of them. Thereafter No 22 began flying 'Rover' sorties, which involved one or two aircraft setting off at low-level for the enemy coast, in search of targets. As usual no escort could be provided on these operations, so once a vessel was sighted a quick attack and an even quicker getaway were essential if enemy fighters were to be avoided. No 42 Squadron was similarly tasked and torpedoed its first ship, a German transport, on 26 October in a Norwegian fjord. The third Beaufort unit, No 217 Squadron, had also started working up at St Eval in Cornwall, commencing operations in October.

The Norwegian and French campaigns had seen a lull in U-boat activity, in the Atlantic at least. In April only seven of 58 merchant ship sinkings were attributable to submarines. But after the conquest of France the Kriegsmarine was able to establish

Above: This No 224 Squadron Hudson was the focus of interest on its return to Leuchars, having been shot up in an encounter with a pair of Dornier flying boats over the North Sea in March 1940. The aircraft landed with its port engine out of action and fuselage streaked with oil. No 224 Squadron had claimed the first enemy aircraft to be shot down by a British-based RAF aircraft, a Dornier Do18 on 8 October 1939. Since then several more German aircraft had been destroyed or damaged by Coastal Command Hudsons, not always without cost. **HU 91237**

bases in the Biscay ports — principally Brest, Lorient and St Nazaire — which provided direct access into the Atlantic, and thus greatly increased the time individual U-boats could spend on patrol in the shipping lanes. The period between July and October 1940 became known to the U-boat crews as the 'happy time'; in those four months 217 merchant ships (most sailing independently) were sunk for the loss of only six submarines. Hitler's announcement of a total blockade on the United Kingdom meant that all merchant ships, whether British, Allied or neutral, could be sunk without warning. In August the head of the German U-boats, Vice-Admiral Karl Dönitz, ordered his crews to make their attacks on the surface and under the cover of darkness. This method had two major advantages — the Royal Navy's ASDIC did not work against surfaced U-boats, and Coastal Command aircraft could not spot them in the dark. The U-boats now had a friend in the skies as well, in the shape of the long-range Focke-Wulf FW200 Condor. From September these aircraft, based at Brest and Bordeaux, were employed to shadow the convoys, relaying information back to U-boat headquarters and on occasions attacking isolated ships themselves.

The Royal Navy's chronic shortage of anti-submarine vessels placed a huge burden on Coastal Command, especially the Sunderlands, of which fewer than 40 were in service. Production of the flying boat was extremely slow and barely able to cope with existing levels of attrition. A rare success occurred on 1 July,

when an aircraft of No 10 Squadron RAAF shared with surface ships in the destruction of *U-26*, using 250lb AS bombs. ASV radar had been fitted to a handful of aircraft, but of even greater importance was the arrival of stocks of aerial depth charges. This thin-cased weapon was basically a version of the Navy's standard 450lb depth charge. It was fitted with a streamlined nose cap and fins and had a much higher charge-to-weight ratio than the AS bomb. Its hydrostatic fuse ensured that it exploded underwater, preventing a premature detonation that could damage, or even bring down, the aircraft dropping it. On 16 August a Sunderland of No 210 Squadron carried out the first aerial depth-charge attack on a U-boat, in this case *U-51*, which was damaged and forced to return to port.

By the autumn of 1940 the U-boats were beginning to co-ordinate their attacks, developing the so-called 'wolf-pack' tactics for which they would become infamous. The successful penetration of British naval codes by German intelligence also conferred a huge advantage. Thanks to this and the additional information supplied by the Condors Dönitz could position his U-boats directly in the path of the convoys. The first successful wolf-pack attack was directed against the 35-ship SC7 convoy on 16 October, when no fewer than 20 vessels were torpedoed by seven U-boats acting in concert. It may have been a 'happy time' for the Germans, but it was the beginning of a critical period for the British. U-boats sank 103 ships in October and another 97 in November. A total of 1,700,000 tons of shipping was sent to the bottom in the second half of 1940. The loss of so many vital cargoes threatened Britain's ability to continue the war.

Unsurprisingly, the Admiralty demanded a massive increase in the number of land-based maritime aircraft. Coastal Command's resources were very obviously insufficient to keep pace with the multiplicity of tasks now required of it.

In addition to their primary anti-submarine and anti-shipping duties, Bowhill's squadrons were still obliged to provide long-range fighter protection for the Royal Navy, assist Bomber Command in mine-laying operations and maintain anti-invasion patrols in the English Channel. It is little wonder that, stretched so thinly and still making do with many unsuitable aircraft, Coastal Command was struggling to make an impact.

The Air Ministry and Admiralty agreed plans to add 15 new squadrons by June 1941, but the supply of aircraft and aircrew was such that this expansion would take place only gradually. No 221 Squadron was formed in November with Wellington bombers, equipped for the maritime role with ASV radar. Nos 502 and 612 Squadrons were re-equipping with another Bomber Command stalwart, the Whitley. By the end of the year three more Blenheim squadrons had been formed or transferred, and No 252 Squadron had been raised to introduce the promising new Bristol Beaufighter into Coastal Command service as quickly as possible. But of much greater significance, new American long-range aircraft — Liberators and Catalinas — were promised for the New Year.

It was at this desperate time that Lord Beaverbrook, Minister of Aircraft Production, famously proposed that Coastal Command be transferred lock, stock and barrel to the Royal Navy. The Defence Committee, chaired by the Prime Minister,

sensibly rejected such a radical idea but reaffirmed that the Navy would indeed remain the dominant partner in the relationship, directing the allocation of resources and retaining operational control of the U-boat war. Yet it hardly needed stating. There were already strong links between the two, thanks largely to the work of Air Chief Marshal Bowhill, who from his first day as C-in-C had fostered close administrative and organisational links with the Senior Service. In fact, the level of co-operation between the Royal Navy and Coastal Command was perhaps the one bright light in an otherwise gloomy outlook.

Below: An Anson of No 502 Squadron, Auxiliary Air Force, undergoing a major inspection at Aldergrove, near Belfast, April 1940. The Anson was powered by a pair of Armstrong Siddeley Cheetah IX engines, developing a modest 335hp at take-off. No 502 was flying intensively at this time, mostly convoy patrols over the Irish Sea and the North-Western Approaches, but, apart from a few attacks on what were assumed to be submerged U-boats, had seen little action. **MH 33968**

Above right: On 13 April 1940 three No 220 Squadron Hudsons flew a reconnaissance patrol along the Norwegian coast between Obrestad and Kristiansand. One of the photographs taken is reproduced here, showing German Heinkel and Blohm & Voss seaplanes at their moorings near Stavanger. During the sortie Flight Lieutenant Harold Sheahen's Hudson was attacked by a twin-engined fighter, possibly a Junkers Ju88C, and sustained damage. His gunner returned fire and, though wounded in the exchange, drove the enemy plane away. On the same day No 233 Squadron lost two Hudsons, shot down as they tried to bomb Stavanger. **C 1223**

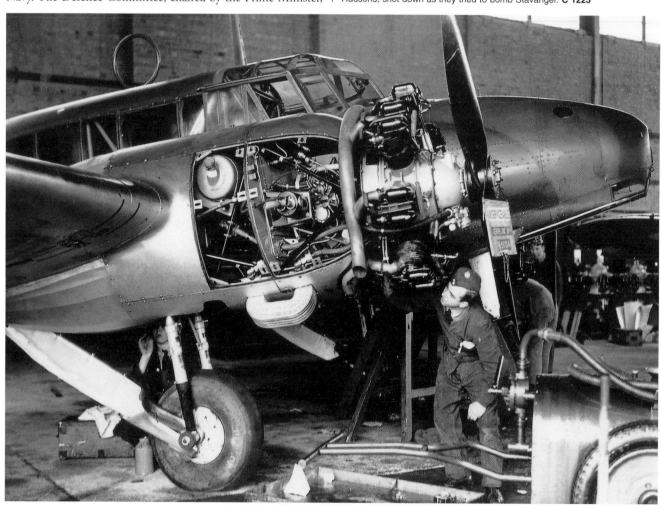

Above: Ground staff carry out routine servicing on Hudson N7303/UA-B of No 269 Squadron, at Wick in northern Scotland, April 1940. The tail has been raised so that the two forward-firing machine-guns in the nose can be sighted. No 269 had only recently begun replacing its Ansons, one of which can be seen in the background. The squadron was employed on North Sea patrols and anti-shipping sorties. In May it would take part in bombing attacks on German forces in Norway. **CH 62**

Left: No 224 Squadron was also heavily involved in the Norwegian campaign. On 23 April 1940 three of its Hudsons were despatched to cover ships of the Royal Navy landing troops and equipment at Andalsnes. One was shot down by 'friendly' anti-aircraft fire from the cruiser HMS *Curacoa*. This aircraft, N7264/QX-Q, was also hit, but was nursed back to Wick with several large holes in its wings and leaking fuel tanks. Its crew is seen here, ruefully inspecting the damage. The Royal Navy was renowned for its poor aircraft recognition, but, in view of the number of Luftwaffe bombing attacks endured by its ships during the campaign, mistakes were bound to occur. **CH 41**

Right: A Sunderland from No 10 Squadron RAAF swoops low over the wake of a destroyer while on a convoy escort 'somewhere in the Western Approaches', April 1940. The first of the many Dominion squadrons to fight during World War 2, No 10 Squadron had been formerly incorporated into No 15 Group Coastal Command on 3 January and was now based at Mount Batten. On 1 July the unit claimed its first shared 'kill' when Flight Lieutenant William Gibson's crew bombed *U-26*, previously damaged by the corvette HMS *Gladiolus*. The U-boat was scuttled by its crew. **FX 4740**

Left: A newly-built Lerwick undergoing final checks at the Saunders-Roe factory at East Cowes, Isle of Wight, May 1940. The Lerwick was introduced into RAF service in July 1939, when two aircraft were delivered to No 240 Squadron at Calshot. Unfortunately these had to be swiftly withdrawn after a host of problems were discovered. Reintroduced in December, this time to No 209 Squadron at Oban, the aircraft were still plagued by poor serviceability and handling problems, and few operational patrols were flown. **HU 91236**

Above: Hudsons of No 206 Squadron, June 1940. The Hudson was replacing the Anson as Coastal Command's standard shore-based aircraft and by the summer of 1940 equipped five squadrons. No 206, based at Bircham Newton in Norfolk, flew anti-shipping sorties along the Dutch and Belgian coasts and during the Dunkirk operation took part in the RAF's desperate attempts to keep the Luftwaffe away from the evacuation beaches. These two aircraft are fitted with additional .303in Lewis guns in the open side windows. A single Browning in a ventral position could also be carried, further enhancing protection in these dangerous skies. **CH 313**

Above right: One of No 206 Squadron's pilots, Flight Lieutenant William 'Willy' Biddell, photographed in his aircraft soon after being awarded the Distinguished Flying Cross for an action on the evening of 31 May 1940. Biddell was leading a trio of Hudsons on patrol near Dunkirk when he sighted a gaggle of Me109s in combat with Fleet Air Arm Skuas. Without hesitating he immediately ordered his flight into the attack and succeeded in driving the Messerschmitts away, damaging at least one of them in the process. Biddell later served with RAF Ferry Command but was posted missing in March 1945. **CH 299**

Right: The gunner on Flight Lieutenant Biddell's Hudson was 19-year-old Leading Aircraftman Walter 'Spike' Caulfield, seen here seated in the aircraft's Boulton Paul turret. Caulfield's fire severely damaged at least one of the enemy fighters. He was awarded the Distinguished Flying Medal. In the first months of the war gunners were part-timers, recruited from the ground staff as and when required, and paid an extra shilling a day flying pay. However, the Air Ministry soon decreed that all aircrew should be specialists, with the minimum rank of sergeant. **CH 301**

Above: Bombing up a Hudson at Bircham Newton, early June 1940. The Hudson's offensive payload of 1,000lb was four times greater than that of the Anson, a typical load comprising four 250-pounders. The aircraft was also significantly faster and had almost twice the range of its predecessor, making it an altogether more effective weapon in Coastal Command's limited arsenal. Also visible in this shot is one of the two forward-firing .303in machine-guns, operated by the pilot. **CH 283**

Above: Beaufort Is of No 22 Squadron lined up at North Coates in Lincolnshire, 19 July 1940. The RAF's first Beaufort was delivered to No 22 Squadron for familiarisation in November 1939, but such were the technical problems and training requirements that operational sorties were not flown until April 1940. The squadron then commenced bombing and mine-laying operations off the enemy coast, but losses due to engine failure and enemy action were heavy. In the summer the crews were taken off 'ops' for a period of further training while modifications were made to their aircraft. **CH 644**

Above: The defensive armament of Beaufort L4461/OA-J. In early-production aircraft the roomy rear turret housed only a single Vickers Gas Operated (VGO) 'K' gun, and operational experience quickly revealed this to be inadequate. Additional guns were fitted as a field modification in beam positions on either side of the fuselage. The port-side gun was mounted in the main entrance hatch, as seen here. Note too the collapsible direction-finding loop on the roof of the fuselage. Despite the casualty rate this aircraft led a charmed life, surviving to be peacefully struck off charge in 1945. **CH 637**

Above left: The crew of this No 10 Squadron RAAF Sunderland featured in a sequence of photographs taken by an official photographer on an operational patrol — reportedly of 14 hours' duration — over the Atlantic in late June 1940. The extensively glazed cockpit could get very hot in the summer months, hence the skipper's appearance! Note the flare pistol cartridges behind the co-pilot's seat, and the aircraft's individual identity letter, 'E', painted on the control panel. **CH 424**

Left: Behind the two pilots the navigator sits at his chart table with the tools of his trade, including plotter, parallel rule and mechanical flight computer. In the early days of the war Coastal Command crews relied almost exclusively on dead-reckoning navigation (using course, speed and time from a known fix to establish current position). Flame and smoke floats — and the wave-tops — were used to assess the inevitable drift caused by fluctuating winds. Radio bearings might be obtained near to land, and astro-navigation could also be used, as long as there was no cloud cover and the navigator was suitably trained. **CH 420**

Above: In the draughty midships section of the aircraft two well-wrapped-up gunners keep watch from their open hatch positions. Scanning the ocean below for the tell-tale signs of a U-boat, or perhaps keeping a look-out for a lone dinghy or ship's boat, was both mentally and physically exhausting. Investigations by Coastal Command scientists later in the war established that after only half an hour of this activity a look-out's effectiveness fell off dramatically. **CH 413**

and next page…

Above left: Galley chores. The vast size of the Sunderland meant that its crews enjoyed a range of facilities unavailable to those of other aircraft. Situated on the lower deck, along with a wardroom and two sleeping compartments, was the galley — complete with cooker, sink and water tank. Each crew had a full-time cook, who doubled as a rigger or gunner. As the official caption to this photograph put it cheerily, 'he can serve a four-course hot meal, or shoot down a German — it's all part of the day's work'! **CH 418**

Left: Off-duty aircrew relax in the aft sleeping compartment. Such scenes were invariably set up by official photographers invited onto the big flying boats. The Sunderland was well loved by its crews, who treated it very much as home from home, sometimes choosing to 'kip aboard' when at base. Later in the war, however, some of this space would be used to store extra bombs and equipment. **CH 556**

Above: Convoy protection. Sunderland L2163/DA-G, one of a pair from No 210 Squadron over convoy TC6, carrying Canadian troops to Britain, on 31 July 1940. The convoy had left Halifax, Nova Scotia, on 23 July and was due to arrive at Greenock on 1 August. This is an original print with a destroyer marked for removal by the censor; in subsequent prints, published many times over the years, the ship does not appear. The Sunderlands stayed on station with the convoy for seven hours before being relieved by aircraft from No 10 Squadron. **CH 825**

Left: An Anson of No 502 Squadron over its charges in the North-Western Approaches, August 1940. For Coastal Command crews actually finding a convoy in the expanse of ocean was a navigational feat in itself, the success of which depended greatly, as always, on the weather. If the convoy had to deviate from its planned course and speed there was still less chance of a successful rendezvous. Furthermore, the ships sailed in conditions of radio silence, so once contact had been made messages could only be exchanged by Aldis lamp. **HU 91238**

Above: The Lerwick was heavily armed, with seven machine-guns in three power-operated turrets. This unflattering view of No 209 Squadron's L7257/WQ-F, recorded at Oban on the west coast of Scotland in August 1940, shows the rear and retractable dorsal turrets to advantage. The stubby Lerwick lacked the majestic grace of the Sunderland and despite the best efforts of its makers remained unreliable and deeply unpopular. The aircraft were grounded again between August and October while further factory modifications were carried out. **CH 864**

Above: A No 210 Squadron Sunderland, L5798/DA-A, being put through its paces for the photographer at Oban, in August 1940. Note the toned-down upper wing roundels, contrasting sharply with the rather conspicuous fin flash. The squadron had detachments at Sullom Voe and Stranraer and was flying reconnaissance patrols off Norway and convoy escorts out into the Atlantic. The forces of nature, rather than the enemy, finally put paid to this particular aircraft, wrecked in a storm at Gibraltar in 1943. **CH 840**

Above: Aircraft maintenance, Coastal style. Another No 210 Squadron Sunderland at Oban, this time DA-J, undergoing its daily servicing routine. One rigger, with a special ladder and a head for heights, is patching the rudder fabric while fitters and flight mechanics concentrate on the various engine checks. Servicing Sunderlands at their moorings was always a challenge, particularly in foul weather. Personnel were ferried to and from the shore in pinnaces operated by the marine-craft sections. **CH 859**

Above: A mooring compartment was situated in the nose of the Sunderland, containing anchor, winch, boat-hook and ladder. The front turret was designed to slide back, enabling the crew to secure the aircraft to a buoy, as demonstrated here. The circle painted on the fuselage just below the cockpit is a gas-detection patch. **CH 847**

Left: Sting in the tail — the Frazer-Nash FN13 rear turret. The Sunderland was the first RAF flying boat to be fitted with power-operated gun turrets, the front having a single Vickers 'K' gun and the rear a more substantial battery of four Browning machine-guns. Good propaganda was made from those occasions when Sunderlands successfully survived attacks by enemy aircraft, the most famous being on 3 April 1940, when a No 204 Squadron aircraft shot down two Ju88s and fought off several more. **CH 854**

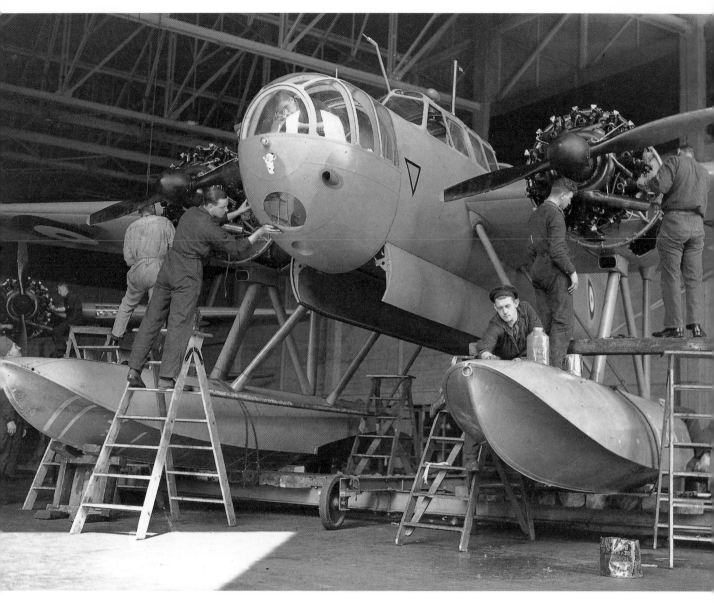

Above:
A Fokker T-VIIIW float-plane of the recently-formed No 320 Squadron, receiving an overhaul at Pembroke Dock, August 1940. The squadron comprised members of the Royal Netherlands Naval Air Service who had escaped with their aircraft after their country was overrun by the Germans. The aircraft sports the Dutch national marking below the cockpit, alongside standard RAF roundels. The Fokkers were put to good use on convoy patrols over the South-Western Approaches until the autumn, when the squadron moved north to re-equip with Hudsons. **CH 1042**

Above right: Chocks away! Anson K6175, part of a No 320 Squadron detachment at Carew Cheriton, near Pembroke Dock, about to set off on an anti-submarine patrol over the Irish Sea in August 1940. A second Anson unit formed from Dutch naval personnel, No 321 Squadron, also operated from here but was merged into No 320 Squadron in January 1941. This particular aircraft was destroyed in a Luftwaffe air raid on 1 October 1940. **CH 1079**

Right:
A cheerful Dutch air gunner in the turret of his Anson at Carew Cheriton. As standard the Anson was fitted with a fixed .303in machine-gun in the nose, operated by the pilot, and a Lewis or VGO 'K' gun in an Armstrong Whitworth turret in the rear fuselage. Some units, notably No 500 Squadron at Detling, experimented with extra weapons, and in a number of encounters with enemy fighters Anson crews actually got the better of their opponents. Such freak events helped raise morale but did nothing to alter the fact that the 'Annie' was obsolete as a combat aircraft. **CH 1081**

Above and below: Two views of *Swee' Pea* — Beaufort L4463/MW-C of No 217 Squadron — on a rainy day at St Eval, Cornwall, in October 1940. The tarpaulin tent (complete with transparent roof panels) erected around the port engine afforded weather protection for at least some of the ground staff. No 217 received its first Beauforts in May 1940, but conversion was slow and the aircraft were not used operationally until September. Meanwhile, the squadron soldiered on with its Ansons until the end of the year. **CH 1599, CH 1600**

Above: Crews from 'A' Flight, No 236 Squadron, sprint to their Blenheim IVFs at Aldergrove, November 1940. The aircraft were fitted with ventral gun-packs and external light-bomb carriers. No 236 was one of four squadrons within Fighter Command transferred to Coastal Command in February 1940 for 'trade protection' duties. The Blenheims performed many tasks, including offensive sweeps, coastal patrols and escorts for RAF and Fleet Air Arm aircraft on bombing and mining sorties. 'B' Flight of No 236 was operating from St Eval at this time. In November Blenheim detachments from Nos 235 and 236 Squadrons at Aldergrove were formed into a new squadron for Coastal Command — No 272. **MH 33978**

Above: The Beaufort was initially employed on mine-laying and bombing operations rather than in its intended torpedo-bombing role. One major problem was that existing torpedoes could not be dropped at the high speeds originally envisaged; instead crews were expected to reduce speed to about 160mph on the run-in — or risk the torpedo breaking up on entering the water. No 22 Squadron flew the first torpedo-armed sorties in September 1940 and achieved a number of successes against enemy ships during the autumn and winter of 1940. L4516, seen here with an impressive array of 'tin fish' at North Coates in early December 1940, was lost later that month when it crashed on take-off and the mines aboard exploded. **CH 1854**

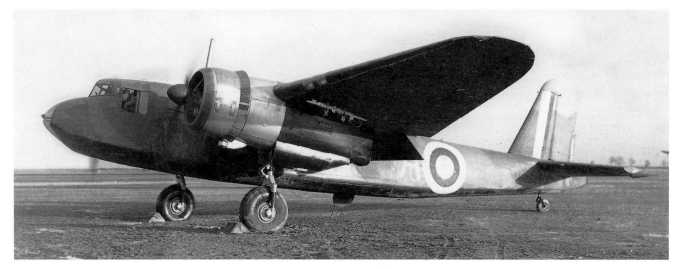

Above: 'Bloody Botha'. The Blackburn Botha achieved notoriety as one of the biggest aviation failures of the war. Despite clear signs that it would be a disaster, the Botha remained in development and finally entered service with No 608 Squadron in June 1940. Only 308 operational sorties were flown before it was restricted to training duties with No 1 Operational Training Unit (OTU) at Silloth, Cumberland, where this photograph was taken in December 1940. **CH 1905**

Above: A Dutch pilot runs up the 880hp Bristol Perseus X engines of a No 1 OTU Botha. Not only was the Botha seriously underpowered, it also suffered from longitudinal instability and control problems and had a worryingly high stalling speed, which makes the decision to switch the type to training duties all the more alarming. Another cause of concern was that the engines blocked much of the navigator's view from his compartment immediately behind the pilot. As a partial cure, curved plexiglass window panels were fitted, as seen here. **CH 1904**

CHAPTER 3

1941

'At this date the squadrons of Coastal had grown in numbers. In 1939 there were nineteen of them. Two years later there were forty. More important than the numbers, the range and hitting power of the aircraft had doubled. The protective frontier behind which our merchant ships could reasonably feel safe was moving out into the Atlantic.'

(Air Chief Marshal Sir Philip Joubert de la Ferté,
Birds and Fishes — The Story of Coastal Command)

Coastal Command began the year having received a trickle of reinforcements and new aircraft, most of which had been transferred from other commands. Some 550 aircraft were now distributed among 33 squadrons, not all of which were home-based. No 200 Group at Gibraltar had been transferred to Coastal Command control, but as yet the only available squadron there was No 202, with Londons and Swordfish floatplanes. No 98 Squadron, operating obsolescent Fairey Battles, and a detachment from No 204 Squadron equipped with Sunderlands were based in Iceland. This strategically important outpost, occupied in May 1940, was a vital acquisition for the British, as it extended the reach of both naval and aerial forces into the North Atlantic. The RAF contingent there was reinforced in the spring, when a detachment of No 269 Squadron Hudsons started operating from Kaldadarnes and the rest of No 204 Squadron moved to Reykjavik. They were joined by a newly-formed squadron of Norwegian personnel, flying Northrop N-3PB floatplanes. At home the handful of Whitleys and Wellingtons now in service were a welcome boost, but there were still only four squadrons of Sunderlands available. Blenheims and Hudsons equipped almost half of the force, but the ageing Ansons and the even more antiquated Stranraer flying boats were still in use.

Bad weather in the Atlantic during the winter of 1940/1 was partly responsible for a decline in the number of ships lost to the U-boats. Another reason was that barely 20 boats were on station during this period, but their numbers soon started to increase, and so did the slaughter. Thirty-nine ships were sunk in February, another 41 in March, and 43 more in April. The North Atlantic had become the U-boats' main hunting ground, especially those based in the Biscay ports. As a consequence the Admiralty began routeing convoys further north in an effort to avoid them. In March Winston Churchill issued his famous 'Battle of the Atlantic' directive, insisting that the war be taken to the U-boats, whether at sea, in their French bases or on the slips at construction yards in German ports. A measure of how seriously the Prime Minister viewed the situation was that Bomber Command, gearing up for its strategic bombing offensive against Germany, was instructed instead to hit ports and factories associated with U-boat production, and to relieve Coastal Command of some of its anti-shipping duties in the North Sea. Coastal Command itself was to concentrate its resources on the Atlantic, specifically the North-Western Approaches (to the estuaries of the Clyde and Mersey), where the bulk of the sinkings was occurring. Several squadrons were re-deployed to bases in Northern Ireland and on the west coast of Scotland.

The re-orientation of Coastal Command's main area of operations from the North Sea to the Atlantic was reflected in organisational changes to its command structure. No 15 Group headquarters, previously based at Plymouth, was moved alongside that of the Royal Navy's new Western Approaches Command in Liverpool. A new No 19 Group was established at Plymouth to control operations in the South-Western Approaches and the Bay of Biscay. No 16 Group and No 18 Group HQs remained at Chatham and Rosyth respectively. From 15 April 1941 the Admiralty was placed formally in charge of the operational direction of Coastal Command, and both air and naval operations continued to be directed from the four Area Combined Headquarters. In each of these the RAF group commander worked alongside (but not under the control of) the naval commander. This 'hand-in-glove' system ensured that the RAF's resources could be brought to bear wherever the Navy was most in need of support, which meant first and foremost convoy protection.

The convoys were at their most vulnerable when outside the limits of air cover. The establishment of bases in Iceland and of Royal Canadian Air Force stations in Newfoundland and Nova Scotia had already gone a long way to reducing the huge area of Atlantic ocean that lay beyond the range of shore-based aircraft and in which surfaced U-boats could operate with relative impunity. But there still existed a stretch of ocean south of Greenland, about 300 miles wide and extending down beyond the Azores, that remained beyond all reach. The shrinking of this so-called 'Atlantic Gap' was of pivotal importance and depended on the procurement of aircraft not only with sufficient endurance to reach far out to sea but also able to remain on station for a useful amount of time. Fortunately for Coastal Command the spring of 1941 saw the first deliveries of new aircraft from the United States that would satisfy these requirements.

The Consolidated PBY-5 flying boat (named the Catalina by the RAF) first entered service with No 240 Squadron in March, followed in April by No 209 Squadron (relinquishing their hated Lerwicks) and No 210 Squadron. The Catalina was slow but had a range of over 2,000 miles, enabling it to patrol for at least two hours at a distance of 800 miles from base. The aircraft destined to become Coastal Command's pre-eminent VLR

Above: Fighting pair. Bristol Beaufighter Is of No 252 Squadron, January 1941. The powerful new Beaufighter had a top speed in excess of 300mph and was heavily armed, with four Hispano 20mm cannon in the lower fuselage and six machine-guns mounted in the wings. No 252 was a new squadron and began flying convoy patrols from Aldergrove in April. Its first victory was a Focke-Wulf FW200 Condor, shot down on the 16th of that month. Introduced as a long-range coastal patrol fighter, the 'Beau' would ultimately carry out all manner of escort and strike roles for Coastal Command, but for now demand was greatest in the Mediterranean, and No 252's aircraft were soon dispatched to Malta. **CH 2747**

(Very Long Range) aircraft was the Consolidated B-24 Liberator, a four-engined land-based bomber well suited to maritime reconnaissance on account of its unrivalled 2,300-mile range. The first Liberators entered service with No 120 Squadron at Nutts Corner, near Belfast, in June, but it would be a while before they were able to make an impact.

While the U-boats represented the major threat, the major German warships were also taking a growing tally of merchantmen. The battlecruisers *Scharnhorst* and *Gneisenau* and, operating separately, the heavy cruiser *Admiral Hipper*, had recently returned to Brest after successful forays into the Atlantic. Now they became the targets of concerted RAF bombing and mining attacks, in which Coastal Command played an important part. During one such strike on 6 April a Beaufort of No 22 Squadron, piloted by Flying Officer Kenneth Campbell, achieved a torpedo hit on the stern of the *Gneisenau*, inflicting serious damage that kept the ship in dry-dock for many months. The Beaufort did not survive the hail of flak put up by the ship, shore-batteries and other ships moored nearby and crashed into the harbour, killing all four men on board. Campbell was awarded a posthumous Victoria Cross.

In May Germany's most powerful warship, the battleship *Bismarck*, in company with the heavy cruiser *Prinz Eugen*, left the Baltic on her maiden cruise and broke out into the Atlantic. After sinking the battlecruiser HMS *Hood* during an action in the Denmark Strait the German ships shook off their pursuers and split up. A huge air search was instigated, and on 26 May the *Bismarck* was spotted by a Catalina of No 209 Squadron and subsequently shadowed by another from No 240. A Fleet Air Arm strike was launched which inflicted vital damage, enabling battleships of the Home Fleet to catch up and batter the great ship into a blazing hulk. On 11 June the pocket battleship *Lützow* (formerly *Deutschland*) was spotted underway in the Kattegat, believed to be preparing for a breakout into the Atlantic. That night, and without an up-to-date sighting report, 14 Beauforts were despatched from Wick and Leuchars; one of these, piloted by Sergeant Ray Loveitt, made a lucky interception and scored a direct hit amidships, forcing the *Lützow* to limp back to Kiel. German capital ships would never again venture out against the Atlantic convoy routes.

Though it was accorded a much lower priority, the campaign against German merchant shipping continued throughout 1941, and with gradually improving results, despite mounting losses and the transfer of aircraft and crews to the Middle East. Most activity involved No 18 Group, whose squadrons flew routine dawn and dusk sorties in the upper North Sea and off the Norwegian coast, sinking a total of 16 ships in the course of the year. No 16 Group, operating between Cherbourg and Wilhelmshaven, claimed another nine merchant vessels, mostly during dusk or night operations. The Beaufort crews of No 22

Above: Lerwick L7265/WQ-Q of No 209 Squadron, in the air over its base at Stranraer, March 1941. Over the winter of 1939/40 No 209 Squadron had resumed operations with its problematic aircraft but lost its commanding officer, Wing Commander J. E. M. Bainbridge, who failed to return from an anti-submarine patrol on 22 February. After a dismal period of service, the Lerwicks were finally withdrawn from operations in May, by which time the squadron had converted to the far superior Catalina. **CH 2362**

Squadron enjoyed particular success on 'Moon Rovers' off the Frisian Islands on clear nights. When Coastal Command's main effort was switched to the North-Western Approaches in the spring of 1941, several Blenheim and Hudson squadrons were transferred away from the East Coast, their place being taken by No 2 Group Bomber Command.

The Beaufighter was beginning to replace the Blenheim IVF as Coastal Command's standard long-range fighter, and six squadrons received the type during the course of 1941. Unfortunately Nos 252 and 272 were transferred to the Mediterranean in April and May, and crews from Nos 143 and 248 Squadrons were also sent overseas later in the year. The remaining aircraft did not fit comfortably into Coastal Command's order of battle. Unable to carry bombs or torpedoes (the all-Beaufighter 'strike wings' lay a long way off in the future) they were of limited use in the anti-shipping role. Their time would come, however.

On 14 June Air Chief Marshal Sir Philip Joubert (de la Ferté) took over as AOC-in-C of Coastal Command. The expansion instigated in the autumn of 1940 had been completed, and at his disposal were 40 squadrons. However, serviceability (never the Command's strong point) was such that only about 80 Hudsons, 40 Whitleys, 36 Catalinas, 20 Wellingtons and 17 Sunderlands were actually available for operations. Over half of these aircraft were equipped with radar. ASV Mk II, an improved version with a sideways-looking capability, had entered service and was able to detect surfaced U-boats at a range of 8-15 miles (depending on height) under operational conditions.

Fortunately for the Command, Joubert was keen to embrace new technology and its application to the anti-submarine war. He quickly recognised the potential of the revolutionary new centimetric radar then under secret development, promising far greater range and resolution. He was also instrumental in providing a solution to another major problem — how to spot surfaced U-boats at night. They could be located by radar, but were usually lost in the surface 'clutter' before a visual sighting was obtained. Two possible designs for aircraft-mounted searchlights were already being tested. Joubert initially favoured the Helmore Light, a fixed, forward-pointing searchlight carried in the nose of an aircraft, but when this was shown to be flawed (its broad diffused beam merely produced glare at sea level) he quickly gave the go-ahead to another device, created by Squadron Leader Humphrey de Verde Leigh. The Leigh Light was belly-mounted and, crucially, could be trained independently of the aircraft's direction or attitude, enabling a U-boat to be held in its beam. The light was ordered into production but would not reach the squadrons until 1942.

By now the operational priorities of Coastal Command's anti-submarine squadrons had changed, with aircraft being used more aggressively. Offensive patrols were being mounted around Britain's shores and over the two main U-boat transit areas —

the Bay of Biscay and the Shetlands–Faeroes–Iceland gap. These 'barrier patrols' reached out to a distance of 350-400 nautical miles and were flown principally by the Whitleys and Wellingtons, while the Sunderlands and Catalinas operated further out over the convoys. Close air escort was removed from those convoys not actually threatened by U-boat attack. Despite the change in strategy, which saw an increase in the number of encounters with U-boats making their slow passage to the Atlantic hunting grounds, Coastal Command aircraft were still spread very thinly, and they were not making kills.

Merchant ship losses continued to rise during May and June, especially off the West African coast, where the U-boats were once again enjoying rich pickings among ships sailing independently. At first only a handful of Sunderlands from the recently-formed No 95 Squadron were available to oppose them in this region, but reinforcements were soon despatched. Joubert ordered the transfer of two more squadrons of Sunderlands and a new Hudson squadron, No 200, to Freetown and Bathurst. Convoying was also instituted. The effect was dramatic — between July and September only two ships were sunk within 600 miles of the African coast.

Undoubtedly the most significant effect in the U-boat war was achieved by 'Ultra' — intelligence provided by codebreakers at the Government Code and Cipher School at Bletchley Park. They had recently penetrated the German Navy's Enigma cipher and from the beginning of June were routinely deciphering intercepted U-boat radio traffic within days or even hours of its being received. A major coup was the capture on 9 May of *U-110*, complete with its intact Enigma machine and codebooks. The constant stream of tactical instructions, sighting reports and operational orders transmitted to and from the U-boats at sea proved to be their Achilles' heel. Armed with this vital intelligence the Admiralty's Submarine Tracking Room was able to re-route convoys away from known U-boat patrol areas and reinforce the escorts of those threatened by waiting U-boats. In July and August only 22 and 23 ships respectively were sunk. It has been claimed that some 300 merchant ships were saved through the re-routeing of convoys — perhaps as decisive a contribution to winning the U-boat war as the growth of Allied air and naval forces.

The Americans, though still neutral, were also making life increasingly difficult for the U-boats. US Navy warships had long been openly reporting the positions of enemy submarines; by September they were escorting eastbound convoys two thirds of the way across the Atlantic and on occasions defending them by force. Allied surface cover now extended the whole way across the ocean, and offensive patrolling by both Canadian squadrons in the west and Coastal Command in the east was forcing Dönitz's crews to operate further and further out into the Atlantic.

But this apparent Allied supremacy over the U-boats proved to be something of a false dawn. Dönitz's force was gradually increasing in strength — numbers rose from 30 operational U-boats in April to 60 in August, of which 39 were in the Atlantic. And Coastal Command was still woefully short of long-range aircraft. Supplies of the new Catalina were slow, and production of the Sunderland even slower. By July No 10 Squadron RAAF was down to only six aircraft, while the only other Sunderland unit in Britain at the time, No 201, could rarely muster more than three aircraft for daily operations. Worst of all, No 120 Squadron, on whose shoulders a great burden of expectation had been placed, was taking a long time working up on its new VLR Liberators. Training requirements and the time needed to complete the various modifications on the aircraft themselves (including the fitting of ASV radar and 20mm gun packs) delayed the squadron's first operational sortie until 20 September. In spite of all this the Air Ministry resolutely refused to transfer some of the new Halifax bombers from Bomber to Coastal Command. Even the Whitleys and Wellingtons were not safe. In October Winston Churchill, perhaps daring to hope that the worst was over in the Atlantic, suggested they be given back to Bomber Command to take part in the strategic bombing offensive. Fortunately for Coastal Command the howls of anguish from the Admiralty were enough to resist the move.

Allied shipping losses rose sharply in September and October (Bletchley Park was struggling with U-boat-position-grid reference codes) but fell off again in November, as winter weather took hold in the Atlantic and the U-boats were ordered to Norway — where Hitler feared a British invasion attempt — and the Mediterranean. Anti-submarine forces based at Gibraltar were reinforced by the Hudsons of No 233 Squadron, and the Bay of Biscay became a focus of activity as U-boats made their way south. There, on 30 November, Flying Officer R. Holdsworth, commanding a No 502 Squadron Whitley, depth-charged a U-boat and was duly credited with the sinking of *U-206*. Unfortunately the submarine he attacked was actually *U-71*, and it escaped unscathed. Holdsworth had failed to break Coastal Command's duck. Aside from the famous capture of *U-570*, which had surrendered to a Hudson of No 269 Squadron on 27 August, during the whole of 1941 Coastal Command aircraft participated in the destruction of only one U-boat (of a total of 35 lost). This was *U-452*, shared between a No 209 Squadron Catalina and an anti-submarine trawler southeast of Iceland on 25 August. Try as it might, Coastal Command had yet to sink a single U-boat unaided.

Above: Beaufort I N1172/AW-S of No 42 Squadron, up from Leuchars, 23-27 March 1941. Though still in short supply, the Beaufort was by now well established in Coastal Command, equipping Nos 42, 22 and 217 Squadrons. The aircraft normally operated in roving detachments, alternating between bases in Scotland, eastern England and the South West. As well as taking part in shipping strikes and 'Rovers' (offensive patrols), the Beauforts dropped mines and bombed ports, oil-storage facilities and airfields. No 42 Squadron's principal hunting ground at this time was the Norwegian coast. N1172 would be lost on a shipping strike in April 1942. **CH 2772**

Right: The Beaufort had been designed to carry four 250lb anti-submarine bombs internally, or, as here, a standard 18in Mk XII torpedo. A cable release mechanism and a detachable air tail were necessary to stabilize the torpedo during the drop, which had to be performed with the aircraft flying perfectly straight and level. The so-called 'spider' fitted to the nose of the torpedo ensured that it exploded even if it struck the target ship a glancing blow. **CH 2424**

Above: Hudson N7326/ZS-F of No 233 Squadron, running up its engines under a threatening sky at Leuchars, March 1941. The squadron had been operating from Leuchars and Aldergrove, seeing anti-shipping action off Norway and patrolling the convoy routes into the Clyde and Mersey. On 28 May 1941 two aircraft, led by the squadron CO, Wing Commander E. C. Kidd, shot down a Heinkel He111. In August the squadron moved to the West Country for operations over the Bay of Biscay. **CH 2429**

Left: The duty officer in the tower at RAF Catfoss in Yorkshire keeps watch while an airman signals to an aircraft using an Aldis lamp, April 1941. Catfoss was home to No 2 (Coastal) OTU, equipped with Ansons and Blenheims. By this date there were four OTUs within Coastal Command's No 17 Group, as well as No 3 School of General Reconnaissance and the Torpedo Training Unit. Another two OTUs were created in the summer, for Hudson and Beaufort conversion. Because Coastal was so stretched the supply of aircraft and, especially, experienced aircrew for the training units was a major problem. **CH 2465**

Top and above: Hudson III T9465, *Spirit of Lockheed-Vega Employees*, was famous as a 'presentation' aircraft, purchased for the RAF from funds raised by workers at the Lockheed-Vega Corporation, at Burbank in California; all those involved in its construction had signed their name somewhere on the inside of the fuselage. These two views show the aircraft being prepared for a sortie at Wick in May 1941, not long after being delivered to No 269 Squadron. A clutch of 250lb bombs are hauled into the bomb bay, after which the crew goes aboard, complete with camera and carrier-pigeon — the all-important 'fifth crew member'. In June No 269 moved to Iceland, taking the 'Spirit' with it. **CH 2648, CH 2649**

Above: A Sunderland of No 10 Squadron RAAF leaving dry dock at Pembroke Dock, May 1941. By this date only two Sunderland squadrons were left in the United Kingdom — No 10 in South Wales and No 201 in the Shetlands. The others were deployed overseas, guarding Allied shipping in an ever widening area of operations: No 95 Squadron had recently been established in West Africa, No 204 was in Iceland, and Nos 228 and 230 were in the Mediterranean. **HU 91251**

Left: Loading a 450lb depth charge onto a No 10 Squadron Sunderland, May 1941. Four such depth charges could be carried, on racks which were run in and out of the 'bomb room' by hand. The standard Amatol-filled naval depth charges were fitted with streamlined nose fairings and tail fins, designed to break away on impact with the water. They were detonated by a hydrostatic fuse, at a depth of 100-150ft. Coastal Command's Operational Research Section soon discovered that this was too deep — a crash-diving U-boat was usually on or just below the surface when the weapons were released. The development of new depth charges with shallow-setting firing pistols therefore became a priority. **HU 91250**

Right: The hunt for the *Bismarck* in May 1941 was a 'maximum effort' involving a host of Coastal Command and Royal Navy units. After destroying HMS *Hood* the German battleship shook off her pursuers and disappeared into the Atlantic, prompting a desperate air search to be instigated. On 26 May Pilot Officer Dennis Briggs of No 209 Squadron, seen here after the event in the cockpit of his Catalina, located the ship 700 miles west of Brest. Other aircraft maintained contact until the Royal Navy could launch a torpedo strike, which crippled *Bismarck's* steering, and stayed on station until British warships arrived to finish her off on the morning of 27 May. **HU 91258**

Above: A Blenheim IVF from No 254 Squadron, based at Aldergrove, June 1941. Coastal Command had 11 Blenheim squadrons at this time, but losses had been appalling; in the first six months of the year 127 aircraft were lost to all causes. Fortunately some squadrons were now re-equipping with more modern types. No 86 was working up on Beauforts, while in July Nos 53, 59 and 608 Squadrons converted to Hudsons, and No 248 received Beaufighters. No 254 Squadron itself continued flying Blenheims on convoy escorts from Northern Ireland until June 1942, when it too re-equipped with Beaufighters. **CH 2898**

Above right: This No 42 Squadron Beaufort crew became the centre of attention after a successful torpedo strike on the heavy cruiser *Lützow* on the night of 12/13 June 1941. Warned by Enigma decrypts that the ship and its escorts were at sea, Coastal Command ordered a strike. Two formations of torpedo-armed Beauforts were dispatched from Wick and Leuchars, but only one aircraft, L9939/AW-W flown by Flight Sergeant Ray Loveitt, made contact in the darkness. His torpedo struck home, putting the ship out of action for several months. Loveitt is seen here (second from left) with his crew: (from left) Flight Sergeants C. T. Downing, A. H. Morris and P. Wallace-Pannell. **MH 7655**

Below: Ground staff prepare to load a torpedo into Beaufort N1015/AW-F of No 42 Squadron, July 1941. Note the rough application of paint to its underside. Camouflage schemes had been the subject of much debate during this period, especially the colours to be used on the undersurfaces of RAF aircraft. The latest official instructions were that Coastal Command torpedo-bombers and land-based general-reconnaissance types should have black undersides, for maximum concealment at night when on bombing sorties. However, since they had to operate by day as well, the squadrons were allowed to apply sky or duck-egg blue to a proportion of their aircraft, as is evident here. **HU 91257**

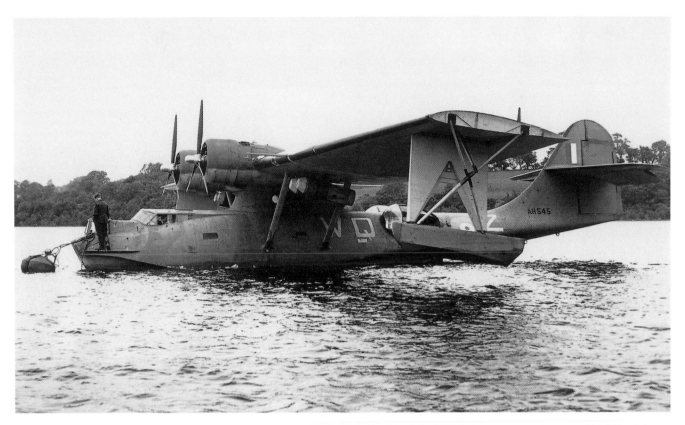

Above: Consolidated Catalina I AH545/WQ-Z of No 209 Squadron, at Loch Erne in Northern Ireland, July 1941. This was the aircraft in which Pilot Officer Briggs (and his US Navy co-pilot and 'special observer' Ensign Leonard Smith) sighted the *Bismarck* on 26 May. Although relatively slow the Catalina had a patrol endurance of 18 hours or longer, thus giving Coastal Command the ability to pursue the U-boats well out into the Atlantic. The aircraft's offensive payload consisted of four wing-mounted depth charges, as seen in this photograph. On 25 August, while operating from Iceland, No 209 Squadron scored its first success, sharing in the destruction of *U-452* with a Royal Navy anti-submarine trawler. **HU 83788**

Above: A Liberator I, AM910, during tests at the Aeroplane and Armament Experimental Establishment (A&AEE) at Boscombe Down in Wiltshire, July 1941. The first six Liberators sent to Britain were unarmed and used for flying ferry pilots back across the Atlantic. The next batch of 20 were fitted with weapons, armour plate, and self-sealing fuel tanks, and went to Coastal Command. These early aircraft lacked power-operated turrets, but were fitted with ASV Mk II radar and four 20mm cannon in a pack below the fuselage. They were the first VLR (Very Long Range) aircraft in the Command. Suitably modified with extra fuel tanks and their armour removed, they could spend two to three hours patrolling at a range of 1,000 miles from base. No 120 Squadron was formed at Nutts Corner, near Belfast, in June 1941 to introduce the new type into service. **ATP 9767B**

Above: As part of the urgent expansion of Coastal Command ordered at the end of 1940 a number of Vickers Wellingtons were made available. They were assigned to the newly-formed No 221 Squadron at Bircham Newton. At first radar-equipped Mk ICs were used, but these were soon replaced by Mk VIIIs, developed specifically for general-reconnaissance and torpedo-dropping duties and fitted with ASV Mk II as standard. By the spring of 1941 the squadron was flying anti-submarine patrols over the North-Western Approaches from Limavady in Ireland. This Mk VIII, W5674/DF-D, was photographed in July 1941 while being used for tests. **ATP 10574B**

Above: Death of a Condor. As the westbound convoy it was stalking steams on in the distance, a Focke-Wulf FW200 is abandoned by its crew, having been shot into the sea by a No 233 Squadron Hudson (serial AM536) on 23 July 1941. Six Germans were picked up by one of the Royal Navy escorts. While shadowing convoys the Condors broadcasted homing signals, to be picked up by waiting U-boats. This co-operation lasted only for a brief period before the U-boats were driven further out into the Atlantic by Coastal Command, well beyond the range of the Condors. **C 1987**

Opposite page: On 27 August 1941 Coastal Command claimed a rare and unusual success when one of its aircraft was instrumental in the capture of a U-boat. A No 269 Squadron Hudson operating from Kaldadarnes in Iceland, flown by Squadron Leader J. H. Thompson, surprised *U-570* as it was surfacing. Thompson dropped a stick of depth charges, after which attack the German crew was seen spilling out onto the casing, waving white flags. The U-boat had been crippled, and deadly chlorine gas was leaking from its flooded battery compartment. These two photographs were taken later by a Catalina from No 209 Squadron, called to the scene along with various Royal Navy vessels. Heavy seas at first prevented a boarding party from reaching the U-boat, but eventually they were able to accept the crew's surrender. The captured submarine was eventually re-commissioned into the Royal Navy as HMS *Graph.* **C 2066, C 2068**

Top: A Hudson V of No 608 (North Riding) Squadron, based at Thornaby in North Yorkshire, September 1941. Since the outbreak of war this auxiliary squadron had operated Ansons, Bothas and Blenheims, before finally switching to Hudsons in the summer of 1941. Its work was similarly varied — convoy protection, air-sea rescue duties and anti-submarine patrols over the North Sea. With the Hudsons came the opportunity for shipping strikes and raids on ports — and an increase in the loss rate. **HU 91256**

Above: Sunderland II W3983/RB-R of No 10 Squadron RAAF, about to be brought out of the water at Pembroke Dock, 3 October 1941.
The Sunderland II, introduced in the spring of 1941, was fitted with more powerful engines and ASV Mk II radar as standard. The characteristic fuselage-mounted 'stickleback' dipole masts and Yagi beam antennae under the wings are visible in this uncensored photograph. This particular aircraft was more successful than most, damaging two Italian submarines during 1942. **CH 16531**

These pages: ABC of the RAF. These examples of Beaufort nose art were recorded on No 42 Squadron aircraft in October 1941. The individual code letters of each aircraft, repeated as standard on the nose for identification purposes, have been extended into suitable names, and distinctly non-standard pictorial representations added by an artistic member of the ground staff. **HU 91245 (Ghoul), HU 91246 (Bulldog), HU 91247 (Churchill), HU 91248 (Adder)**

Above: Flight Sergeant J. L. Burnham, 'flight fitter' on a No 10 Squadron RAAF Sunderland, calculating the aircraft's fuel consumption with the aid of a slide-rule, October 1941. With the advent of four-engined aircraft in Bomber Command the Air Ministry created a new crew category of flight engineer, whose task was to relieve pilots of the many routine engine checks and adjustments. Coastal Command Sunderland squadrons had already made their own provision, and many air gunners were trained to carry out this function. This photograph was stopped by the Air Ministry censors as it shows the then secret CRT (cathode-ray tube) indicator unit for the ASV Mk II radar. **CH 17163**

Above right: An upsurge in U-boat activity off the West African coast prompted an urgent deployment of Coastal Command Sunderlands to the area, starting with the newly-formed No 95 Squadron in March 1941, followed by No 204 Squadron in August. Operations were conducted from Freetown in Sierra Leone and Bathurst in The Gambia, the aircraft flying long patrols out into the South Atlantic or up along the coast as far as Gibraltar. This No 204 Squadron Sunderland I, T9041, is seen at Bathurst in the autumn of 1941. Like many early-mark Sunderlands sent to this theatre, it has been retro-fitted with ASV radar. It was eventually lost in June 1942 after ditching on an air-sea rescue sortie. The West African-based Sunderlands failed to sink any U-boats but were successful in deterring further convoy attacks. Coastal Command formally relinquished control of the units in West Africa in October 1941. **CM 6557**

Right: Aussies at play at Pembroke Dock, October 1941, with Sunderland I T9072/RB-F looming in the background. The official caption writer made the most of this juxtaposition: 'Rugby football is another favourite with the Australians, and they play a robust as well as clever game. It's to be hoped that the fierce looking scrum didn't bump into the Sunderland in the background. They might have damaged it!' In the event the aircraft was lost on 5 December 1941, when an engine failure caused it to crash into the sea off Holyhead. **CH 4355**

Above: A Northrop N-3PB of No 330 Squadron at Iceland, October 1941. This Coastal Command squadron was formed from Norwegian personnel, displaced after the invasion of their country, and trained in Canada. Equipped with US-built Northrop float-planes originally ordered by the Norwegian Government, the squadron began operations in June 1941, flying anti-submarine patrols and convoy escorts from various bases on the island. **CS 33**

Above: No 269 Squadron's most-photographed Hudson, T9465 *Spirit of Lockheed-Vega Employees*, bathed in early-morning sunshine while being readied for an anti-submarine patrol from Kaldadarnes, October 1941. No 269 was based here in southwest Iceland until March 1943, when the River Olfusa burst its banks and flooded the low-lying airfield. The squadron relocated to nearby Reykjavik and eventually returned to Britain in January 1944. **CS 112**

Above: Beaufighters of No 248 Squadron at St Eval, October 1941. The aircraft in the foreground is T4776/WR-F. No 248 had started converting to Beaufighter ICs in July, and a detachment was now operating from Cornwall on interception patrols over the Isles of Scilly and the northwest coast of France. Coastal Command's only other operational Beaufighter squadron at this time was No 143, flying convoy escorts and fighter patrols from Sumburgh in the Shetlands. **HU 26300**

Above: Armstrong Whitworth Whitley V Z6475/WL-D of No 612 Squadron at St Eval, October 1941. The first Whitleys to see service with Coastal Command were those of Nos 58 and 77 Squadrons, Bomber Command, on various temporary attachments in 1939 and 1940. No 502 Squadron was the first Coastal squadron to convert to the type, exchanging its Ansons in October 1940. No 612, another auxiliary squadron, followed suit at the beginning of 1941, flying convoy escorts and anti-submarine patrols from northern Scotland. In October a detachment moved to St Eval for operations over the Bay of Biscay. **HU 26481**

Top: The first Canadian squadron in Coastal Command was No 407 'Demon' Squadron, formed at Thorney Island in May 1941 and — after an interim period with Blenheims — equipped with Hudsons. It became operational in September, flying 'Rovers' and anti-E-boat patrols over the southern reaches of the North Sea. In this shot, taken at North Coates on 2 November 1941, aircrew and ground staff gather around a YMCA tea car for 'char and a wad'. The aircraft on the right is that of the CO (note the pennant), Wing Commander H. M. 'Monty' Styles. **HU 91252**

Above: No 407 Squadron pilot points out some minor flak damage to the fuselage of Hudson AM728/RR-V. The official caption was suitably colourful: 'There is something about the "V" sign that gets the Nazis worried. Back from a scrap over the North Sea this machine shows signs of close combat.' On 22 December the aircraft did not escape so lightly and was shot down on a strike near the Dutch island of Texel. **HU 91253**

Right: Pilot Officer J. F. 'Jimmy' Codville of No 407 Squadron RCAF makes an appropriate Churchillian gesture in the cockpit of his Hudson. The previous night Codville's crew had claimed two hits on a 6,000-ton merchant ship during an attack on a convoy off the Dutch coast. Sadly he was reported missing soon after this photograph was taken, his aircraft shot down by a German night-fighter on 5 November. The Demon Squadron lost six crews on anti-shipping strikes before the year was out. **HU 91254**

Above: Beaufort I W6537/OA-F of No 22 Squadron starting up at St Eval, December 1941. The accumulator trolley in the foreground supplied the necessary electrical power to the aircraft and was disconnected once the engines were running. Unlike other Beaufort squadrons, No 22 fitted a Vickers 'K' gun in the nose compartment of its aircraft, to be used for flak-suppression during low-level attacks. This Beaufort was one of the lucky ones, surviving service with three operational squadrons before being scrapped in 1944. **CH 17131**

Above: Time for tea. The Air Officer Commanding-in-Chief of Coastal Command, Air Chief Marshal Sir Philip Joubert (right), enjoys a 'cuppa' with some of his pilots from a YMCA tea car, 8 December 1941. The tea car was one of five supplied by the British War Relief Society in the United States, hence the presence of the American pilot in the centre. The date is significant — on the other side of the world the Japanese had launched their attacks on British and US possessions in the Far East and Pacific. The war was entering a new phase, and, for a while at least, the USA would need to devote its attention and resources to its own defence. **CH 4110**

CHAPTER 4

'The offensive policy in the Bay of Biscay, certain technical improvements such as the provision of the Leigh searchlight to facilitate night attacks, and the arrival of the Very Long Range Liberator, had produced a great improvement in the results of the anti-U-boat war.'

(Air Chief Marshal Sir Philip Joubert de la Ferté,
Birds and Fishes — The Story of Coastal Command)

Hitler's foolish declaration of war on the United States on 11 December 1941 finally brought the world's greatest industrial nation firmly into the Allied camp. Winston Churchill remarked that he slept the sleep of the saved, knowing that with the productive might of the Americans galvanised there could no longer be any doubt about final victory. The Axis nations were doomed, and all that was now required was 'the proper application of overwhelming force'. But for now there were major obstacles to overcome. At a time when attention was fixed on the calamities befalling them in the Far East, the Americans were also to receive a terrible initiation into the realities of the U-boat war, one that the Royal Navy and Coastal Command were powerless to prevent.

In January Dönitz ordered some of his larger long-range U-boats to the western Atlantic, where they took up station off the North American coast for Operation 'Paukenschlag' ('Drum Roll'). In this new theatre of operations the U-boats enjoyed a second 'happy time', preying on merchant shipping — tankers in particular — sailing alone and undefended. Night attacks were greatly aided by the absence of a blackout ashore, and vessels silhouetted against the lights of coastal towns and cities made easy targets. The massacre off the East Coast — and to a lesser extent in the Caribbean — continued until the early summer, by which time the US Navy had finally put its house in order and adopted convoying and other defensive measures. Coastal Command's No 53 Squadron, posted to the West Indies, operated its Hudsons as far south as the Orinoco River and did much to limit the damage inflicted on shipping in the Caribbean and off the coast of South America.

For the British too, early 1942 was a period of almost unremitting disaster, with dramatic Japanese conquests in the Far East, Malta under siege and the war in North Africa going badly. The need for reinforcements in these theatres was acute and had major ramifications for the home-based RAF in general and Coastal Command in particular. As well as the continuing drain of crews posted overseas from his operational training units, Joubert would lose three Catalina squadrons and eventually all four Beaufort squadrons. The Air Ministry promised to restore aircraft numbers from future supplies, but in the short term Bomber Command would once again have to lend squadrons to make up the shortfall.

And U-boat numbers were steadily increasing. In February 1942 some 101 were operational, and this number would double before the year was out. Set against this was the increased output of merchant shipping from British and American yards. The Battle of the Atlantic had become a race; Dönitz knew only too well that if he was to win, his U-boats would have to sink Allied shipping faster than it could be replaced. In his favour were new developments in the intelligence war. At the beginning of the year German naval intelligence cracked the cipher used for routine communications between Allied escort ships and until the summer of 1943 was able to read much of this radio traffic. Another advantage enjoyed by Dönitz for most of 1942 (though of course utterly unknown to him) was that Bletchley Park had been left floundering by a new, more complex variant of the naval Enigma used for communications between the U-boats and their headquarters in France. As a result the Allies were often blind when it came to assessing U-boat numbers and dispositions, and convoy re-routeing was then impossible.

The sinkings off the USA in the first half of 1942 precipitated a crisis in the Battle of the Atlantic. In the first three weeks of Operation 'Paukenschlag' 40 ships were sunk. More U-boats were sent west across the Atlantic, their operations extended using 'milch cow' supply submarines. In March a total of 95 Allied and neutral ships were lost to U-boats. In April 74 were sunk, in May 125, and in June 144 vessels were torpedoed — the highest monthly total of the war. By the middle of 1942 eight out of ten merchantmen lost were being sunk by U-boats. In crude tonnage terms it looked like Dönitz was indeed winning the race. In the same period only 22 U-boats were destroyed, none by Coastal Command. By July the second 'happy time' was effectively over, and the U-boats were ordered back into the mid-Atlantic, to prey once again on the convoys to Britain.

Meanwhile, Coastal Command's anti-shipping campaign was producing disappointing results. Only six enemy merchant ships were sunk during the first four months of the year, and losses were severe among the Hudson crews bearing the brunt of operations off southern Norway and the Dutch coast. Twenty-four aircraft failed to return during March and April alone. Joubert was so appalled by the figures that in June he ordered a cessation of low-level attacks in favour of medium-level bombing (from 4,000ft). Unfortunately the lack of an effective bombsight meant that attacks carried out in this manner were ineffective, though less costly. The continuing loss of experienced crews to overseas postings, or to instructional duties at the training units, further contributed to the worrying reduction in efficiency now apparent in the anti-shipping squadrons.

Nor were operations against enemy capital ships any more successful. On 12 February the infamous 'Channel Dash' took place, when the *Scharnhorst*, *Gneisenau* and *Prinz Eugen* broke out of Brest and headed through the Channel in a successful bid to return to home waters. It was an embarrassing fiasco for the British, whose contingency plan to deal with this not unexpected move failed miserably. On that day of bungled activity, Coastal Command's Beauforts based at St Eval and Thorney Island struggled in appalling weather to launch their attacks, as did the Hudsons of No 407 Squadron RCAF, but the lateness in detecting the enemy force (the ships were due south of Dover when the alarm was finally raised) and communication problems between the bombers and their fighter escorts meant that their efforts were totally wasted.

Shortly after this set-piece two of the Beaufort squadrons (Nos 22 and 217) were posted to the Far East in a vain attempt to shore up British fortunes there. They were replaced by two Handley Page Hampden squadrons, Nos 144 and 455 RAAF, transferred from Bomber Command. Two existing Coastal Command squadrons, Nos 415 and 489, had also begun converting to this aircraft, no longer required for the strategic bombing offensive but with some remaining potential for anti-shipping work. The Hampdens started out with bombing and mining operations, then transferred to anti-submarine patrols over the Bay of Biscay as they built up their experience. Later they participated in 'Rovers' and shipping strikes off southern Norway and the Dutch coast.

The remaining Beauforts got another chance to prove themselves on 17 May, when a maximum effort was launched

Below: Ground staff prepare a No 233 Squadron Hudson for flight in freezing conditions at Thorney Island, 19 January 1942. The 'hot air van' has been brought in to warm up the engines and de-ice the cockpit windscreen. No 233 Squadron's main task at this time was anti-submarine work, and detachments were based at St Eval and at North Front, Gibraltar. In July the whole squadron relocated to Gibraltar, where it remained until 1944. **CH 4772**

against the *Prinz Eugen*, reported steaming south from Trondheim towards German waters. Twenty-seven torpedo-bombers were escorted by a contingent of Beaufighters and Blenheims for flak suppression, while a force of Hudsons was also sent to carry out a diversionary bombing attack. Despite attempts at co-ordinating the strike, the results were predictably bad. The battlecruiser successfully avoided the torpedoes, and several RAF aircraft were shot down by the barrage of flak put up by the ship, or by Luftwaffe fighters scrambled from Norway. It was the last major operation for the UK-based Beauforts. No 42 Squadron was sent overseas in June, followed by the air echelon of No 86 in July.

Action against shipping in the North Sea was always regarded as a sideshow. The war against the U-boat was paramount; Air Chief Marshal Joubert's prime concern during this period was to extend his Command's reach westwards into the Atlantic, particularly the dreaded 'Gap', in which the wolf-packs were able to operate undisturbed by Allied air patrols. The shortage of suitable aircraft remained a fundamental problem. No 120 Squadron was still the only one equipped with VLR Liberators and was far from up to strength — barely half a dozen aircraft were normally operational. The Americans, keen to build up their own bomber force, were resisting calls to supply more, so Joubert again requested supplies of four-engined bombers from Bomber Command. The Avro Lancaster had recently entered operational service, but its use was jealously guarded by Bomber Command's uncompromising new C-in-C, Air Chief Marshal Sir Arthur Harris. The Admiralty echoed Joubert's demands, by now only too aware of Coastal Command's importance in the U-boat war.

In June the Air Staff finally ordered Harris to release a detachment of Lancasters for maritime use. Six aircraft from No 44 Squadron were sent to Nutts Corner, and nine from No 61

Squadron went to St Eval in July. Joubert was also offered extra Whitleys and Wellingtons, more readily cast off from the bomber force. The new squadrons included No 58, permanently transferred from Bomber Command, and four others on temporary attachment. They made a useful contribution to the barrier patrols being flown over the Bay of Biscay, where as a result of improvements in tactics and technology the tide was about to turn.

A key factor was the work of the Operational Research Section, set up at Northwood in March 1941 to analyse scientifically all aspects of Coastal Command's activities, especially the tactics used against the U-boats. The details of individual attacks — height and speed of the aircraft, angle of attack, depth-charge settings and a host of other factors — were now being routinely examined. From this scrutiny emerged revised tactical instructions and the practical advances necessary to carry them out successfully. Rear-facing cameras to record attacks and an effective low-level bombsight were two such products of Operational Research.

Another long-overdue development was the creation of an effective airborne weapon. The standard Amatol-filled naval depth charge, set to explode at its minimum depth of 50ft, had proved little more effective than the anti-submarine bombs in use at the beginning of the war. But the advent of compact 250lb versions filled with the vastly more powerful explosive Torpex, and set to explode just below the surface, meant that even a near miss would often be lethal to a crash-diving U-boat.

Also crucial was the development of the Leigh Light, but by the middle of 1942 this was still only fitted experimentally to a handful of No 172 Squadron Wellingtons. The device made its operational debut on the night of 3/4 June, when four aircraft flew sorties over the Bay. A number of Spanish fishing boats were successfully illuminated after being picked up on the ASV radar. More usefully, the Italian submarine *Luigi Torelli* was also caught on the surface, successfully depth-charged and forced to limp into a Spanish port for repairs. Then, on the night of 5/6 July, Pilot Officer Wiley B. Howell, an American, surprised a U-boat west of La Rochelle, straddling it with depth charges. *U-502* went down with all hands, the first enemy submarine to be sunk by a Wellington and the first to be sunk using the Leigh Light. Significantly, though no-one knew it at the time, it was also the first to be sunk by an aircraft of Coastal Command acting alone. Another U-boat, *U-751*, was the first to be sunk in daylight after separate attacks on 17 July by a Whitley and a Bomber Command Lancaster.

At this mid-point in Coastal Command's war a significant milestone had been reached, one that signalled the beginning of a major turnaround in the Battle of the Atlantic. In the first six months of 1942 only 22 U-boats had been sunk by Allied forces. But during the last half of the year a total of 65 U-boats failed to return from their patrols, with aircraft — British, American and Canadian — accounting for a growing number.

Coastal Command's heightened effectiveness against the U-boats in the latter half of 1942 was due not only to tactical refinements and scientific advances but also to increases in its numerical strength. Production of the Sunderland was now healthy enough to keep pace with losses and equip several new units as well. No 461 Squadron was formed in April using surplus Australian crews from No 10 Squadron RAAF. Two new Canadian squadrons, Nos 422 and 423, also received Sunderlands, although the former was restricted to ferrying duties until 1943. Nos 119 and 246 Squadrons started Sunderland operations in the autumn, but both were destined to be disbanded in the New Year. The Wellington was also establishing itself as an important constituent of Coastal Command's anti-submarine force. In September a detachment from No 172 Squadron at Wick was expanded to form No 179 Squadron. Both were equipped with the Wellington GR VIII, the first version of the aircraft to be designed specifically for the general-reconnaissance role.

The supply of American aircraft was also improving, albeit gradually. In July No 224 Squadron began exchanging its Hudsons for Liberator IIIs, commencing operations in October, during which month they sank two U-boats. No 59 Squadron also received Liberators at this time but kept them only until the beginning of 1943. No 86 Squadron, which had lost most of its Beaufort crews to the Middle East, also re-equipped with Liberators but was screened from operations and used instead for crew training. Two other Hudson squadrons, Nos 206 and 220, had started converting to another American land-based bomber, the Boeing B-17E, known to the RAF as the Fortress IIA. No 206 Squadron flew its first Fortress operations from Benbecula in the Hebrides in September, and sank *U-627* on 27 October. No 220 Squadron, at Ballykelly in Northern Ireland, switched to the Fortress IIA in July after a six-month period of operations with the much inferior Fortress I, a type rejected by Bomber Command after some unsuccessful attempts at high-altitude daylight bombing.

While the U-boat war in the Atlantic necessarily dominated operations during 1942, Coastal Command was now also committed to supporting convoys taking war *matériel* and supplies to the Soviet Union. The first of these left Britain in August 1941, using a route via Iceland and thence east around northern Norway to Murmansk and Archangel. At first there was no need for air support, but in 1942 the Germans began concentrating U-boats, warships and aircraft around Alten Fjord, near the North Cape of Norway. Liberators of No 120 Squadron in Iceland and Catalinas of No 210 Squadron based in the Shetlands provided long-range reconnaissance and anti-submarine cover as far east as they could, but the distances involved meant that little time could be spent over the convoys themselves. It took a Catalina 10 hours to reach the North Cape from the Shetlands. As a result the Russians agreed to play host to a number of RAF detachments. Six Catalinas from Nos 210 and 240 Squadrons were based on Lake Lakhta, near Archangel, by the time convoy PQ17 sailed in July, but they could do little to prevent the disaster that occurred when the convoy was ordered to scatter and virtually destroyed by air and submarine attack.

The threat posed by German capital ships, especially the battleship *Tirpitz*, against the northern convoy route had

Above: Hudson III T9459, part of No 233 Squadron's detachment at North Front, with the famous Rock of Gibraltar providing a backdrop, March 1942. The Hudsons flew convoy patrols off Portugal, around the northwest African coast and eastwards into the Mediterranean. Several U-boats were attacked, and on 14 November *U-605* was sunk. Vichy French fighters were an additional menace to Coastal Command aircraft operating in this area. T9459 was lost after ditching in the sea east of Gibraltar in October 1942. **CM 6629**

directly precipitated the destruction of PQ17. To counter it a detachment of Hampden torpedo-bombers from Nos 144 and 455 Squadrons was temporarily transferred to Vaenga in northern Russia, from where they carried out anti-shipping and anti-submarine patrols. Their presence may well have helped deter German warships from putting to sea against the next outbound convoy, PQ18, which sailed in mid-September, but the U-boats and Luftwaffe torpedo-bombers were still active and sank three and 10 merchant ships respectively. By the late autumn the RAF crews had returned to Britain, having turned

their aircraft over to the Russians. Coastal Command would never again be as active in northern waters.

The Hampden squadrons achieved a degree of success on torpedo-bomber operations off the coast of Norway, but the aircraft itself was a stop-gap and never the answer to Coastal Command's pressing need for an effective anti-shipping aircraft. Both the Hudson and Beaufort were too slow and too vulnerable for low-level sorties, especially now that enemy merchantmen were being accompanied by an increasing number of heavily-armed escort ships. The Beaufighter looked altogether more promising, however, and in September Joubert's superiors at the Air Ministry finally granted his request for torpedo-equipped versions to be made available.

The Beaufighter made possible a new form of anti-shipping operation, in which specialist torpedo-bomber ('Torbeau') and anti-flak ('Flakbeau') squadrons co-ordinated their attacks for maximum effect. This strike-wing concept had been in the

Above: No 204 Squadron also had a detachment at Gibraltar in the spring of 1942. One of its Sunderlands, L5798/KG-B, is seen being hauled back into the water following maintenance work. This veteran Mk I was delivered to the RAF in 1938 and had seen service with Nos 210 and 201 Squadrons before being transferred to No 204 in July 1941. It wears an early-war camouflage scheme and is not fitted with radar. The aircraft was damaged beyond repair in a storm in September 1943. **CM 6527**

planning stage for some time and was to a great extent influenced by the experiences of aircrews operating against Axis convoys in the Mediterranean. The key was for flak-suppression attacks to be carried out immediately before the main torpedo assault went in, thus ensuring the defences were in a suitably confused and disrupted state when the Torbeaus were at their most vulnerable. A further advantage was that the Beaufighter was fast enough for single-engined fighter escorts to provide effective cover during these operations — something that was impossible in the case of the ponderous Hampdens.

In November the first Beaufighter strike wing was formed at North Coates. The wing comprised three Beaufighter squadrons — No 254 with torpedo-carrying 'Torbeaus' and Nos 236 and 143 Squadrons in the 'anti-flak' role. Unfortunately their first operation, against a convoy off the Hook of Holland on the 20th, was a disaster. The attack force, made up of 24 aircraft from Nos 236 and 254 Squadrons, failed to rendezvous with its Spitfire escort and on reaching the target found it to consist of only one merchantman and several escorting armed trawlers. To make matters worse, enemy fighters also arrived on the scene. In the ensuing battle three RAF aircraft were shot down, and seven others badly damaged, for negligible results. The North Coates Wing was withdrawn for further much-needed training.

By late 1942 the areas where the U-boats could operate with relative impunity, safe at least from air attack, had shrunk considerably. They had been driven well away from Britain's shores and were now being harried almost continuously in the

Above: Hudson V AM853/OY-K of No 48 Squadron, on an air test from Wick, April 1942. As well as convoy and anti-submarine patrols, the squadron flew hazardous anti-shipping strikes off the Norwegian coast. In the first three months of the year 20 aircraft were lost to weather and enemy action. This particular Hudson escaped the attrition, going on to serve with No 459 Squadron in the Mediterranean. **COL 183**

transit areas, especially the Bay of Biscay, across which the majority were obliged to travel on their way to and from port. To help them run the gauntlet, many boats had been fitted with an electronic receiving device called 'Metox', designed to detect ASV radar emissions at anything up to 30 miles away — long before the submarine itself could be picked up by a searching aircraft. 'Metox' enabled many submarines to dive before they could be spotted, especially at night, when the U-boats were more likely to be found on the surface. The Luftwaffe also was lending a hand, with Ju88C-6 fighters flying long-range patrols out over the Bay. During September and October they shot down 15 Coastal Command aircraft. Their predatory activities were countered to some extent by Coastal Command Beaufighters from Nos 235 and 248 Squadrons, transferred to No 19 Group and despatched on long-range fighter sweeps.

In November 1942 the Allies embarked on Operation 'Torch', the landing of Anglo-American forces in Vichy-French Morocco and Algeria. Coastal Command was heavily involved in protecting the huge troop convoys as they headed towards the Mediterranean. In preparation for the assault a number of

squadrons were sent to Gibraltar in advance. No 210 Squadron took its Catalinas south in October, followed by two squadrons of Hudsons (Nos 500 and 608) and the Leigh Light Wellingtons of No 179 Squadron. In their absence Bomber Command and a handful of American heavy bomber units 'filled in' as best they could closer to home. 'Torch' was a resounding success, especially for Coastal Command and the anti-submarine forces based on Gibraltar. The U-boats completely failed to disrupt the landings — and paid a high price in the attempt.

The year proved to be one of crisis for the Allies at sea. A grand total of 1,664 ships were sunk in all theatres, of which U-boats were responsible for 1,160; in the North Atlantic alone they torpedoed no fewer than 1,006 vessels (5,471,222 tons). Dreadful though this toll undoubtedly was, it was offset to some extent by the increasing number of U-boats falling victim to Allied forces. The steady build-up of air power at sea had become perhaps the most significant factor in the Battle of the Atlantic. In the second half of the year the combined Allied air forces had been responsible for half of all U-boat sinkings. And Coastal Command, after a slow and frustrating start, was at last contributing to the attrition, destroying 13 U-boats through its own endeavours between July and the end of December. The pendulum of the U-boat war had by no means swung completely in the Allies' favour, but it would be fair to say that, from this point on, Dönitz's 'Grey Wolves' were as much the hunted as the hunters.

Left: Beaufort I X8931/L2 of No 5 OTU, based at Chivenor in Devon, April 1942. This aircraft was one of the many delivered straight to an OTU rather than to an operational squadron. In fact Beauforts were in such demand that, by this time, more were serving in training units than with front-line squadrons. Some were also used to train Beaufighter and, later, Mosquito crews. No 5 OTU carried out all aspects of Beaufort training except torpedo-dropping itself, for which the Torpedo Training Unit at Turnberry in Scotland was responsible. **CH 5963**

Right: Torpedo-armed Beaufort IIAs of No 42 Squadron at Wick, April 1942. Coastal Command was in the process of relinquishing its Beaufort force, as units moved to overseas theatres where the need for anti-shipping aircraft was considered greater. No 22 Squadron was the first to go, sent to the Far East in February (its aircraft were retained in the Mediterranean until April). No 217 was despatched eastwards in March, its crews absorbed by No 39 Squadron on Malta. No 42 flew out to Malta in June and operated there until November, before moving on to India. Finally, in July No 86's air echelon was also transferred to Malta, while the rest of the squadron stayed at home to convert to Liberators. **CH 17806**

Above: By the spring of 1942 the Beaufighter IC had supplanted the Blenheim IVF as Coastal Command's principal long-range fighter. It was far better suited to a range of tasks, including escorts, convoy patrols, shipping 'recces' and night intruder operations. Numbers were limited though by the steady drain of aircraft and crews to the Middle East. Nos 235, 236 and 248 Squadrons were all active at this time, operating from bases in Scotland, the Shetlands and the West Country. This aircraft, T4916/LA-T, was on the strength of No 235 Squadron. **COL 187**

Above: Pilots from No 248 Squadron photographed with Beaufighter IC T4712/WR-G, during a press visit to Dyce in Scotland, 17 April 1942. They are (from left): Sergeant G. P. Windsor from Brisbane, Squadron Leader D. L. Cartridge, Sergeant R. F. Hammond — another Australian — and, looking suitably rakish, Squadron Leader R. E. G. Morewood. No 248 was flying regular patrols off the Norwegian coast and escorting Beauforts on anti-shipping strikes. **HU 91255**

Above: Hampden I AT137/UB-T of No 455 Squadron RAAF, May 1942. This Australian squadron had transferred from Bomber Command in April and was now based at Leuchars, where it was training for a new torpedo-bombing role. Progress was slow, however, and the first strike operation did not take place until September, carried out by a detachment operating from Vaenga in the Soviet Union. This aircraft was not to see action, being destroyed in a ground fire at Leuchars in June. **COL 182**

Above: Whitley VIIs of No 612 Squadron at Reykjavik, May 1942. The squadron had moved to Iceland in December 1941, flying convoy escorts and anti-submarine patrols over the North Atlantic. A detachment was also maintained at St Eval for Bay operations. Based on the standard Whitley V, the Mk VII was fitted with extra fuel cells and ASV Mk II radar, although in this photo the aerial arrays have been neatly censored. **CS 249**

Above: The heavy cruiser *Prinz Eugen* was torpedoed and severely damaged by a British submarine off Norway in February 1942. On 16 May she sailed from Trondheim in an attempt to reach her home port in Germany for further repairs. Coastal Command organised a strike for the following evening involving 12 No 42 Squadron Beauforts, including the Mk IIA seen here with its crew preparing for the operation. The Mk IIA was powered by American Pratt & Whitney Twin Wasp engines and was fitted with an improved 'Blenheim-type' rear turret with twin Brownings. **C 2450**

Above: The strike force was accompanied by four Beaufighters from Nos 235 and 248 Squadrons, for flak suppression during the Beauforts' run-in, and six Blenheim IVs from No 404 Squadron RCAF, including the one in this photograph, whose task was to draw some of the cruiser's fire by simulating torpedo attacks. No 404 'Buffalo' Squadron had formed in May 1941 and had flown many sweeps and escort 'ops' over the North Sea. In September it re-equipped with Beaufighters. **C 2449**

Above: Hugging the Norwegian shore, the *Prinz Eugen* makes her way southwards while under attack from Coastal Command aircraft on the evening of 17 May 1942. The heavy anti-aircraft barrage she put up shot down three of her attackers, and a follow-up wave was intercepted by enemy fighters and suffered heavy losses. No hits were scored by the RAF, and the ship made Kiel safely the following day. **C 2448**

Above: As well as anti-submarine patrols, the Norwegians of No 330 Squadron in Iceland also flew the occasional mercy mission in their Northrop N-3PB float-planes. In May 1942 they were called upon to ferry a seriously ill woman from her home in a remote bay to hospital in Reykjavik; she is seen here being gently assisted from the rear seat of the aircraft after the flight. No 330 Squadron moved to Scotland at the end of the year to re-equip with Sunderlands. **CS 221**

Above: U-boats were not the only threat to the convoys in northern latitudes. A watch had to be kept on the Arctic pack-ice, the extent and composition of which varied depending on the time of year. To this end No 269 Squadron in Iceland flew regular 'ice patrols' over the Denmark Strait between Iceland and Greenland. A sequence of photographs illustrating these activities was taken in May 1942, starting with this portrait of an unidentified Hudson crew about to climb aboard their aircraft. **CS 166**

Right: The navigator at work in his confined space in the nose of the Hudson. As ever, the sortie depended on extremely accurate navigation — if the crew were unsure of their own position they could not hope to plot the extent, direction and rate of drift of the ice with any degree of precision.
One problem peculiar to these extreme latitudes was the effect of the earth's magnetism on the aircraft's compass, which might show an error of up to 10 degrees. **CS 172**

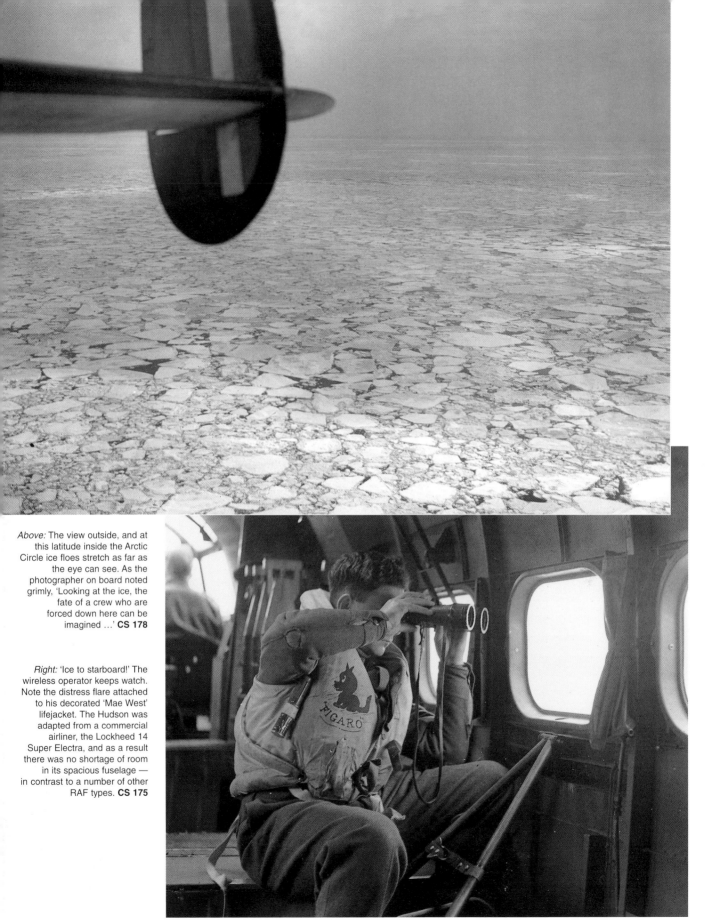

Above: The view outside, and at this latitude inside the Arctic Circle ice floes stretch as far as the eye can see. As the photographer on board noted grimly, 'Looking at the ice, the fate of a crew who are forced down here can be imagined ...' **CS 178**

Right: 'Ice to starboard!' The wireless operator keeps watch. Note the distress flare attached to his decorated 'Mae West' lifejacket. The Hudson was adapted from a commercial airliner, the Lockheed 14 Super Electra, and as a result there was no shortage of room in its spacious fuselage — in contrast to a number of other RAF types. **CS 175**

Above left: U-71 dives amidst a hail of machine-gun fire from a No 10 Squadron RAAF Sunderland in the Bay of Biscay, 5 June 1942. The Sunderland crew dropped eight 250lb depth charges, but the U-boat chose to fight it out on the surface for several minutes before submerging. Badly damaged and unable to continue its patrol, it was forced to limp back to La Pallice. The Sunderland too was hit several times during the exchange and also headed back to base. On the way the aircraft was shot up again, this time during an inconclusive encounter with an FW200 Condor! **C 2611**

Left: In June 1942 the *Spirit of Lockheed-Vega Employees* — the Hudson III presented to the RAF by Lockheed workers and operated by No 269 Squadron in Iceland — was forced to crash-land on an isolated sand-spit after running into a storm. Only slightly damaged, the aircraft was dismantled by a salvage crew during a seven-week operation and brought back by ship for repairs. It was later transferred to No 161 Squadron — a 'special duties' unit involved in agent-dropping over Europe — and was eventually struck off charge in July 1943. **CS 202**

Above: Members of the Women's Auxiliary Air Force (WAAF), formed in June 1939, made up an increasing proportion of the RAF's ground staff as the war progressed, thereby releasing men for other duties. This group was photographed during the overhaul of a Whitley V bearing No 51 Squadron codes in June 1942. As a result of experiments by operational research scientists, Coastal Command aircraft were now painted predominantly white, with only their top surfaces camouflaged in dark green and grey. This scheme conferred a significant degree of invisibility against the sky and clouds in northern latitudes. No 51 Squadron was on detachment from Bomber Command and from May to October 1942 flew anti-submarine patrols over the Bay of Biscay. **CH 5831**

Right: Rescue mission. Landing a Sunderland on the open ocean was fraught with danger, as its thin hull and planing surfaces were never designed to withstand a pounding from large waves and heavy seas. Despite this many crews alighted to pick up the survivors of shot-down aircraft. One such incident occurred in the Bay of Biscay on 13 July 1942, when a No 77 Squadron Whitley crew was picked up by a Sunderland from the newly-formed No 461 Squadron RAAF. This scene was one of a number reconstructed later back at Mount Batten for the benefit of an official photographer. **CH 6156**

Below: The skipper of the Sunderland was No 461 Squadron's English CO, Wing Commander Neville Halliday, seen here handing out cigarettes to his relieved and hungry new passengers in the official re-enactment. On 12 August he attempted a similar rescue, but this time his aircraft bounced on the wavetops and broke apart. Halliday and all but one of his crew perished. The Wellington crew for whom they sacrificed their lives were picked up several days later by a motor launch. **CH 6160**

Above and left: On 17 July 1942 *U-751* was attacked and crippled in the Bay of Biscay by a Whitley of No 502 Squadron. Later it was spotted by an Avro Lancaster from No 61 Squadron, Bomber Command, one of those seconded to Coastal Command for anti-submarine sweeps. The Lancaster delivered its load of depth charges and anti-submarine bombs in two attacks, and the submarine eventually slid beneath the waves for the last time. The first photograph was taken from the Whitley and shows the U-boat disabled, unable to dive and circling — apparently out of control. The second was taken looking back over the Lancaster's starboard wing, shortly before the U-boat sank. Unknown at the time, this was Coastal Command's first unaided daylight kill!
C 3143, HU 91243

Above: In the summer of 1942 No 59 Squadron was flying anti-shipping patrols along the Dutch coast, mostly at dusk or on moonlit nights. During one such operation on 6 August this Hudson IIIA, FH426, piloted by Squadron Leader Phil Evans, was hit by flak and struggled home to North Coates with a huge hole in its starboard wing. Its crew can be seen standing by the tail of their aircraft. Later that month No 59 Squadron came off operations and began converting to anti-submarine Liberators. Meanwhile, FH426 was repaired and passed on to other units. It failed to return from an operation with No 233 Squadron on 28 December 1942. **CH 6721**

Above: A Beaufighter IC, T4836, of No 236 Squadron, based at Oulton in Norfolk, August 1942. The squadron code ('ND') and individual aircraft letter have been obscured by the censor. As was common practice with many other hard-worked Coastal Command squadrons, detachments from No 236 alternated between aerodromes in Cornwall, Scotland and the East Coast, wherever demand was greatest. The squadron's tasks ranged from escorting anti-submarine aircraft over the Bay of Biscay to shipping 'recces' off Norway and night-intruder operations over France. **CH 6723**

Above: Battle of the Bay. No 19 Group Headquarters and No 502 Squadron at St Eval were featured in a sequence of photographs taken 23-26 August 1942, depicting the planning and execution of a typical anti-submarine patrol. Here, Air Vice-Marshal Geoffrey Bromet, AOC No 19 Group, and his SASO (Senior Air Staff Officer), Group Captain H. Brackley, review U-boat positions in the new underground Area Combined Operations HQ at Mount Wise, Plymouth. Prints taken during successful attacks on U-boats are pinned to the wall above. **CH 7025**

Above: You cut and I'll spread! Somewhat further down in the RAF's hierarchy, two WAAF cooks at St Eval share the unenviable task of preparing rations for the crews rostered to fly. Thermos flasks were squadron property, and those in the photo are all marked accordingly — No 502's stand ready on the left, and those belonging to No 58 Squadron, also based at St Eval at this time, can be seen lining the shelf on the right! Note too the box of oranges, an imported luxury often unavailable, and a small reminder — if one were needed — of the importance of convoy protection. **CH 7039**

Left: The second pilot of a No 502 Squadron Whitley VII gives his skipper a helpful push as they climb aboard their aircraft, at the start of an anti-submarine patrol. The camera just visible poking out of the hole in the fuselage was used to record the effectiveness of U-boat attacks — a standard F24 camera was mounted vertically and fitted with a mirror to give a rear-facing view. Its automatic shutter-release mechanism was switched on at least 5sec before the depth charges were released and kept on for at least 15sec afterwards, during which time the pilot maintained his altitude and heading. **CH 7043**

Right: On board the Whitley as it sets out on patrol. In the cramped cockpit the skipper consults with his navigator while the second pilot flies the aircraft. Anti-submarine patrols were normally flown at 5,000ft, with cloud cover employed to give maximum concealment. In conditions of low-lying haze, when U-boats had a limited horizontal view, the aircraft were instructed to fly much lower, once again to minimise the chance of being spotted first. **CH 7048**

Right: Tired but safely home. Twelve hours after setting off the Whitley crew is back at St Eval, being interrogated by the intelligence officer. No contacts were reported. Indeed, Coastal Command failed to sink a single U-boat in August, but from this point on its fortunes began to change. Three submarines were sunk in the Atlantic in September, and six more in October — roughly a third of the total number destroyed by Allied forces. By concentrating its efforts on the U-boat transit areas, of which the Bay of Biscay was the most important, Coastal Command was operating with increasing effectiveness — and at last killing U-boats. **CH 7056**

This page: This striking sequence was taken by the rear-facing camera of a No 77 Squadron Whitley during its attack on *U-705*, caught on the surface in the Bay of Biscay on 3 September 1942. Depth charges can be seen splashing into the water just ahead of the crash-diving U-boat and then exploding, sending up great plumes of water and spray. The lethal range of the Torpex-filled 250lb depth charge was 19ft, and experience had shown that a 'stick spacing' of 100ft was the most effective, with the centre of the stick aimed approximately 50ft in front of the U-boat's conning tower. Low-level bomb-sights were now available, but many Coastal Command crews were accustomed to carrying out attacks by eye, at an optimum height of 50ft. The depth charges were set to detonate at 25ft, approximately 5sec after release. The final shot was taken on a subsequent pass and shows the disappearing U-boat leaving a patch of oil and air bubbles. It sank with all hands. **HU 91244, HU 91259, HU 91260, HU 91261**

Above: Liberator III FK222, August 1942. The Liberator was the aircraft on which so much depended at this stage of the Battle of the Atlantic, yet due to an unwillingness on the part of the Americans to divert resources from their bomber forces it was not available in anything like sufficient quantity. By September 1942 No 120 Squadron was operating three different variants from Northern Ireland and Iceland, but still only a handful of true VLR aircraft were available to cover the Atlantic 'Gap'. Nos 59 and 224 Squadrons commenced operations with Liberator IIIs in October, but these were anti-submarine sorties over the Bay of Biscay rather than convoy patrols in the mid-Atlantic. The standard Mk III had an endurance of about 12 hours but could be modified to VLR status by stripping out equipment and fitting extra fuel tanks. **ATP 10951A**

Above: Sunderland II W3984/RB-S of No 10 Squadron RAAF, October 1942. This was not a view to be offered to an enemy aircraft. Despite the 'flying porcupine' propaganda, the giant aircraft was acutely vulnerable to fighters, particularly the Ju88Cs of V/KG 40 operating over the Bay of Biscay. If no cloud cover was available a Sunderland crew's only hope if attacked was to fly as close to the water as possible, thus covering the aircraft's unprotected undersides. Later versions were more heavily armed, with forward-firing machine-guns in the fuselage and extra weapons fitted in side hatches. It is believed that at least 40 Sunderlands were shot down by enemy fighters during the war. **CH 7501**

Top and above: The shattered remains of Liberator III FL910/H of No 224 Squadron, wrecked while attempting to land at Predannack in Cornwall, 20 October 1942. The aircraft, captained by Flying Officer David Sleep, was crippled by one of its own depth charges during an attack on a U-boat southwest of Ireland. One of six DCs released exploded on contact with the submarine's casing, the blast ripping into the Liberator's tail. Sleep and his crew battled with the badly damaged flight controls for the rest of the trip back to base but lost control on final approach. **CH 7709, CH 7710**

Above: 'Any landing you can walk away from …' The crew of Liberator FL910 were fortunate to escape with their lives. Here Flying Officer Sleep (left) poses with three members of his crew, grim-faced but relieved after surviving their ordeal. They are (from left): Flight Sergeant Ron Johnson (air gunner), Sergeant Sam Patterson (second pilot) and Sergeant George Lenson (flight engineer). The target of their attack had been *U-216*, sunk with all hands. **CH 7708**

Above: The other American four-engined bomber used by Coastal Command was the Boeing B-17 Flying Fortress. This example, Fortress IIA FK197, was photographed at Prestwick in October 1942 after its Atlantic delivery flight. By this date the Fortress IIA (based on the B-17E) was in service with Nos 206 and 220 Squadrons, operating from Benbecula in the Outer Hebrides and Ballykelly in Northern Ireland respectively. The Fortress did not have the range of the Liberator (maximum endurance was about 11 hours), but it was an effective anti-submarine weapon. **CH 6885**

Above: Two bomber squadrons, Nos 304 (Polish) and 311 (Czech), were transferred to Coastal Command in the spring of 1942. Equipped with Wellington ICs, they flew anti-submarine patrols from Dale and Talbenny in South Wales. This No 304 Squadron aircraft and crew were photographed in November 1942. The Polish national marking is proudly displayed below the cockpit. No 304 Squadron operated Wellingtons of various marks for the rest of the war, but No 311 converted to Liberators in 1943. **HU 91262**

Above: Daily inspection for a Liberator III of No 224 Squadron at Beaulieu in Hampshire, December 1942. Because numbers were limited, Coastal Command Liberators destroyed only four U-boats during 1942, Nos 120 and 224 Squadrons claiming two apiece. This was about to change, however. With more aircraft finally becoming available, and operations extended to the U-boat transit areas as well as the Atlantic convoy routes, the Liberator squadrons would eventually become the most successful U-boat-killers in the RAF. **CH 8089**

CHAPTER 5

1943

'Headquarters at Northwood were looking forward to a spring campaign in 1943 that was to give Admiral Dönitz many sleepless nights. Ten-centimetre ASV was available, the Leigh Light was working well, and the strength of the Command was growing apace.'

(Air Chief Marshal Sir Philip Joubert de la Ferté,
Birds and Fishes — The Story of Coastal Command)

Until now the advantage in the U-boat war had been won and lost several times, but in the late spring of 1943 the initiative would pass finally and irrevocably to the Allies. An increased output of ships and aircraft, new technological developments and the years of hard-won experience all finally came together, shifting the strategic and tactical balance dramatically. During some of the greatest convoy battles of the war — in which Coastal Command played a decisive role — a huge defeat would be inflicted on the U-boats, and the Battle of the Atlantic effectively won.

All this lay in the future when, on 5 February 1943, Air Marshal John Slessor replaced Joubert as AOC-in-C of Coastal Command. As with several other Allied commanders appointed to high rank at this time in the war, Slessor would benefit handsomely from the measures already put in place by his predecessors. At his disposal were 43 RAF squadrons, of which five were training or forming, and another seven units on loan from Bomber Command, the Fleet Air Arm, the USAAF and US Navy. In the primary anti-submarine role were nine Sunderland squadrons, six Wellington squadrons, three squadrons of Fortresses and three of Catalinas. The Handley Page Halifax was now also entering service with Coastal Command, equipping Nos 58 and 502 Squadrons. VLR Liberators were still in short supply, and Nos 120 and 86 Squadrons were unable to put up more than 18 aircraft between them. The Liberator supply problem was to be a constant preoccupation for Slessor, as it had been for Joubert before him.

As Slessor took the reins of Coastal Command, there was good news from Allied intelligence. Bletchley Park had finally cracked the more complex Enigma naval cipher which had defeated it for 10 months during 1942. Subject to the sometimes substantial delays between receiving and decoding material, the codebreakers were once again able to eavesdrop on the high levels of radio traffic between the U-boats and their headquarters and finally to inform the Admiralty's Operational Intelligence Centre that its own Atlantic cipher had long been compromised by the Germans. From September 1943 Allied naval intelligence was reading German Enigma decrypts within 24 hours.

Another vital technical development on the Allied side, perhaps the most important in the 'shooting war', was

centimetric radar, first developed in 1940 but only now ready to enter RAF service. Based on the cavity magnetron and operating on a wavelength of less than 10cm, this powerful new radar offered a far superior range and resolution compared with earlier metre-length sets. Unfortunately for those fighting the Battle of the Atlantic, priority was initially given to Bomber Command, where it was used for navigation and blind-bombing (and known as H2S). However, the continuing U-boat threat finally persuaded the Air Ministry to sanction an over-water version, designated ASV Mk III, for Coastal Command. In March the first operational sorties with the new sets were flown by Leigh Light Wellingtons of No 172 Squadron, and other squadrons were soon equipped. ASV Mk III gave 360° cover, could detect a surfaced U-boat within 12 miles, and crucially, its emissions were invisible to 'Metox'.

'Metox' had given the U-boats a definite advantage in late 1942. This and the onset of Atlantic gales during the winter months protected the U-boats, and there were few sightings and no kills in January 1943. In February No 19 Group, whose 'patch' it was, made a concerted effort to intercept all U-boats crossing the Bay of Biscay — the 'Valley of Death', as the German U-boat crews had morbidly christened it. It was decided to focus day and night patrols on specific areas of the Bay, astride the main submarine transit routes. Operation 'Gondola' lasted for 12 days and resulted in one kill, that of *U-268*, sunk by a Leigh Light Wellington of No 172 Squadron on 19 February.

The 'Battle of the Bay' continued during March and April with Operations 'Enclose', 'Enclose II' and 'Derange'. Coastal Command's entire anti-submarine strength was drafted in, flying hundreds of sorties in various designated patrol areas. Centimetric radar was now installed in about 70 aircraft — Liberators, Halifaxes and Wellingtons. For night attacks at least 30 ASV Mk III/Leigh Light Wellingtons were available. The result was a substantial increase in both sightings and attacks. Only one U-boat was definitely sunk (*U-332*, by a Liberator of No 224 Squadron on 29 April), but at least two others were so badly damaged that they were unable to continue their patrols and had to head back to port. The constant harassment slowed the passage of the U-boats to their patrol areas and did nothing for the peace of mind of their crews, many of whom returned with hair-raising tales of sudden attacks and narrow escapes.

The situation improved once they were out in the mid-Atlantic, and it was here that Dönitz was concentrating his force, hoping that a continuation of his wolf-pack attacks would inflict a major reverse on the Allies. Despite the losses incurred running the transit routes in the Bay, approximately 50 U-boats were operational and inflicting grievous losses on the convoys. In March no fewer than 108 ships were sent to the bottom. The biggest battle was fought in atrocious weather around the convoys SC122 and HX229 during 16-20 March. The U-boats began their attacks on the two convoys when they were some 900 miles from land and initially beyond the limits of air cover. During the night of 16/17 March 12 ships were sunk or damaged. On the following day the first VLR Liberators from No 120 Squadron arrived, attacking six U-boats, and only one ship was lost. More ships were sunk during the night, but the Liberators were back again after daybreak on 18 March and once again successfully disrupted the wolf-packs. By now the convoys had sailed to within range of other Coastal Command aircraft, and a Fortress of No 206 Squadron sank *U-384* on 19 March. At this point the U-boats withdrew. They had sunk a total of 21 ships from the two convoys and would have wreaked even greater havoc had it not been for the handful of VLR Liberators reaching the area when they did. Never had the importance of long-range air cover been more graphically illustrated.

The supply of Liberators was debated at the Allied Atlantic Convoys Conference in March. The conference agreed on establishing Canadian and American VLR Liberator squadrons in Newfoundland — a move that went a long way towards closing the 'Atlantic Gap'. The Americans also finally agreed to release substantial numbers of the aircraft to Coastal Command, but British attempts to establish a unified command structure over the whole Atlantic theatre of operations were fiercely resisted. Admiral King, C-in-C of the US Fleet, had eyes only for the Pacific theatre and would not agree to having one Allied commander in sole charge of all Atlantic air operations — a position that would, of course, have been filled most suitably by the AOC of Coastal Command.

The gradual strengthening of Coastal Command was mirrored by that of the surface forces. By early 1943 the Allies had just enough escort vessels to create 'support groups', whose function was to rush to the defence of threatened convoys and actively seek out U-boats wherever they were detected. By the beginning of April three escort carriers — two British and one American — had become available for North Atlantic operations, their small, crowded decks home to anti-submarine Swordfish and Avengers of the Fleet Air Arm. The carriers accompanied the convoys or sailed with the roving support groups, and they too were instrumental in closing the 'Gap'.

Despite their successes in March the U-boats were suffering their own, increasingly severe attrition; in that month 15 were destroyed, six of them by Coastal Command. In April another 16 U-boats failed to return from their patrols. Six of these were sunk by the RAF in the Atlantic, and one (*U-227*) was successfully depth-charged north of the Faeroes by a Hampden of No 455 Squadron. Meanwhile, Allied shipping losses in April fell to half the catastrophic March total. The Battle of the Atlantic had reached a turning point.

In early May Convoy HX237, with the carrier HMS *Biter* on station with the escort group and extensive cover from VLR Liberators from Newfoundland and Iceland, got through after losing only five ships. The anti-submarine forces co-operated well, and five U-boats were destroyed. On 12 May No 86 Squadron Liberators for the first time deployed a new weapon

— an acoustic homing torpedo known for security reasons as the Mk 24 mine. *U-456*, the unlucky recipient of this first attack, was severely damaged and later finished off by surface forces. The next convoy, SC170, was even more fortunate. Attempts by up to 17 U-boats to launch attacks near Iceland were disrupted by continuous air cover, and not a single ship was lost; six U-boats were sunk, four by Coastal Command. In the middle of the month 10 separate convoys lost only six out of a total of 370 ships. On 22 May, by which date 33 U-boats had been destroyed, Dönitz ordered his crews to withdraw from the North Atlantic. In total 41 U-boats were sunk during May 1943 — a disaster from which the Kriegsmarine would never recover.

The situation in the Bay of Biscay had also reached a crisis point. The impact of anti-submarine operations in March and April had forced Dönitz to order his crews to stay submerged at night and to surface (to recharge batteries) only during the day, when they had a better chance of spotting enemy aircraft. He also instructed his crews not to crash-dive if attacked but to fight back against their tormentors using the light anti-aircraft weapons now fitted to 'bandstands' on the submarines' conning towers. This change of policy suited Slessor, who welcomed the extra opportunity to attack and sink U-boats, even if it meant that more of his own aircraft would be shot down in the ensuing firefights. He therefore abandoned night patrols and concentrated all his resources on daylight operations.

In June Dönitz ordered his U-boats to cross the Bay in groups, in order to bring a heavier weight of firepower to bear against aerial attackers. This made the U-boats more formidable but also easier to find and forced Coastal Command to operate in greater numbers so that aircraft could reinforce each other when required. Operations 'Musketry' and 'Seaslug' involved aircraft from Nos 19 and 15 Groups respectively, flying mutually supportive patrols. Once one or more U-boats were sighted the other aircraft were called in before attacking. Slessor reinforced No 19 Group for these operations and made good use of two USAAF anti-submarine Liberator squadrons that arrived at St Eval in July.

Coastal Command operations in the area continued to be threatened by the Luftwaffe. With the U-boats ever more vulnerable, the long-range fighter unit V/KG 40 had stepped up its efforts to intercept anti-submarine aircraft, and the air war over the Bay had escalated. In May and June Ju88s destroyed 14 Coastal Command aircraft, including two Sunderlands — each of which shot down one of its attackers before succumbing. The Beaufighters of No 248 Squadron had been providing a measure of protection and had been joined by detachments of Fighter Command Mosquitos flying 'Instep' patrols. In May a detachment from No 235 Squadron brought its Beaufighters back to Cornwall from Scotland to reinforce No 248 as air activity increased. The Beaufighters and Mosquitos made the most of opportunities to use their formidable armament offensively. On 14 June Mosquito IIs from No 307 Squadron, Fighter Command, strafed a group of five U-boats; two were damaged so severely that they had to return to port. By August another Coastal Command Beaufighter squadron, No 143,

Above: This well-worn Sunderland III, W4004/Z of No 10 Squadron RAAF, has just been winched out of the water in preparation for an overhaul at Mount Batten, January 1943. The aircraft fell victim to the Luftwaffe on 17 May, when it was shot down by a Ju88C of V/KG 40 over the Bay of Biscay. Its crew of 12, led by Flight Lieutenant M. K. Kenzie, were all lost. **CH 16148**

Above: Sunderlands of No 246 Squadron riding a gale at their moorings at Bowmore, in the Western Isles of Scotland, February 1943. During one of the worst storms ever experienced in the area, crews were forced to stay aboard their aircraft for several days, keeping the engines running to maintain position and in one case climbing out onto the wing to act as counterweights. They were kept supplied by stores wrapped in parachute bags and lashed to dinghies, paid out on a line from nearby tenders. One aircraft was beached during the storm, but damage was minimal. The squadron, only recently formed, was destined to be disbanded in April, and its aircraft redistributed to other units. **CH 10187**

Above: A Hudson of No 320 Squadron undergoing routine maintenance at Bircham Newton on 24 February 1943. The squadron, manned largely by Dutch naval personnel, had spent many months employed on anti-shipping strikes and 'Rovers' off the enemy's North Sea coast, losing 21 aircraft in the process. The only other home-based Coastal Command squadron still operating Hudsons at the beginning of 1943 was No 407, and that was in the process of converting to Wellingtons. **CH 8825**

seconded from the North Coates Wing, was operating in the long-range-fighter role over the Bay.

As the Battle of the Bay intensified during the summer of 1943, more new weapons were deployed by Coastal Command. The 35lb hollow-charge anti-submarine bomb was first used on 3 July by a No 224 Squadron Liberator. Squadron Leader P. J. Cundy's aircraft was hit by return fire during the attack, but *U-628* was sent to the bottom. Five days later, the redoubtable Squadron Leader Terrence Bulloch, also of No 224 Squadron, further strengthened his reputation as Coastal Command's top 'sub-killer' when he used a specially modified Liberator against *U-514*. Bulloch's aircraft was armed with depth charges, a homing torpedo and four 60lb rocket projectiles mounted on the forward fuselage. All three were used in a devastating attack,

and the U-boat sank with all hands. In all 12 U-boats were sunk by aircraft in the Bay during July.

On 2 August Dönitz rescinded the 'fight back' order. During the 97 days that it had been in force at least 28 Allied aircraft had been shot down, but over the same period 20 U-boats had been lost and almost as many damaged — a poor exchange as far as the Kriegsmarine was concerned. Henceforth the U-boats would sail alone, hugging the Spanish coast as far as possible. Their 'Metox' receivers were also removed, the Germans believing incorrectly that Coastal Command aircraft could home in on it. Once again Slessor altered his search patterns accordingly, and there followed a new series of day and night patrols, under the operation name 'Percussion', stretching as far down as the Spanish coast and involving Gibraltar-based aircraft as well.

While the Battle of the Atlantic reached its climax in the spring and summer of 1943 Coastal Command's anti-shipping effort continued, albeit on a much smaller scale. Thanks to very effective intelligence-gathering (through agents and photo-reconnaissance flights) the routes and times of convoys, especially those in the North Sea, were by now known in such detail that strike aircraft on 'Rovers' were almost assured of finding targets. Nearly all shipping off the Dutch, German and Norwegian coasts now sailed at night, so most Coastal Command sorties were flown at dawn or dusk.

A major new Beaufighter variant was now entering Coastal Command service. The Mk X was the most prolific and the first truly multi-role version of the aircraft, able to carry rockets, bombs or torpedoes (the less numerous Mk XI was similar, but without the torpedo fitment). The new Beaufighters started re-equipping units in the spring and were also allocated to the Hampden squadrons, whose aircraft were no longer suitable for the anti-shipping role. The Hudson too was finally bowing out after heroic service. The last UK-based unit was the Dutch No 320 Squadron, which transferred to No 2 Group Bomber Command in mid-March. Like everyone else, Air Marshal Slessor wanted Mosquito fighter-bombers, but the aircraft was in short supply and Coastal Command last in line, inevitably. A few Mk IIs were delivered before the end of the year, going to No 333 (Norwegian) Squadron, for specialist reconnaissance missions, and later No 248 Squadron.

Below: This No 320 Squadron Hudson VI, EW899, was almost lost after colliding with an enemy aircraft 500ft above the North Sea on a night sortie in February 1943. Despite extensive damage to the tail and fuselage the aircraft was nursed back to base by its severely shaken crew. The enemy aircraft was believed to have hit the sea and been destroyed. By now it was abundantly clear that the Hudson was no longer suited to such hazardous work, and in March No 320 Squadron was withdrawn from 'ops'. It was later transferred to No 2 Group Bomber Command and re-equipped with B-25 Mitchells. **CH 8731**

In April 1943 the North Coates Strike Wing re-entered service after four months of training, during which it had also trained to use 3in rocket projectiles. On 18 April it flew its first strike, against a large northbound convoy off the Dutch coast. Twenty-one Beaufighters were despatched with an escort of Spitfires, Typhoons and Army Co-operation Command Mustangs. A large Norwegian ship was sunk and others damaged for no loss. Eleven days later another strike sank three ships for the loss of one aircraft. The Strike Wing was finally in business.

Rocket projectiles gave the Beaufighter squadrons an added and much-needed punch, especially in view of the continuing shortage of torpedoes. On 22 June Nos 236 and 143 Squadrons used 60lb RPs operationally for the first time, but crews found aiming difficult and failed to press home their attacks. From July a more aerodynamic 25lb armour-piercing head was used instead and proved a much more effective weapon, as it was easier to aim and could penetrate a ship's hull below the waterline. Between June and December 1943 the weapon was responsible for five of the nine ships sunk by Nos 16 and 18 Groups.

Despite these early successes Slessor regarded anti-shipping operations as an expensive luxury — the North Coates Strike Wing was flying an average of only two operations per month. He would have preferred to use more of his Beaufighters in the long-range fighter role over the Bay of Biscay, but the Ministry of Economic Warfare was quick to point out that a reported decline in available targets was a direct result of the Strike Wing's attacks and a measure of its success. Moreover, with enemy

convoys increasingly compelled to sail under the cover of darkness, they were also vulnerable to night assaults by Royal Navy motor torpedo boats. The North Coates Wing operated successfully for the rest of the year. In November it was joined by another, formed at Wick and comprising No 144 Squadron with Torbeaus and No 404 Squadron RCAF in the anti-flak role. Both squadrons had been operating together for some months, their 'beat' being the Norwegian coast.

Between the end of May, when the U-boats were driven from the North Atlantic, and August 1943 not a single Allied ship had been lost on the northern convoy routes. Dönitz's crews had been operating further south in the Azores, off the South American coast and in the Caribbean. In August, after much political and diplomatic pressure, the Portuguese allowed the

British to begin building an airfield on Terceira Island in the Azores, thus plugging the last remaining significant air gap. But in the same month Dönitz made another attempt to disrupt the North Atlantic routes, sending out a wolf-pack of 28 boats. After some initial successes the pack was hounded during September and October by VLR Liberators and strong surface escorts, including MAC ships (Merchant Aircraft Carriers) sailing with the convoys. Twenty U-boats were sunk, of which eight were destroyed by Coastal Command Liberators.

In October the Fortresses of Nos 206 and 220 Squadrons began operating from Lagens airfield in the Azores, where they were soon joined by a detachment of Hudsons from Gibraltar-based No 233 Squadron. Together they formed No 247 Group and proved their worth by sinking supply

U-boats in mid-Atlantic and deterring attacks on Gibraltar-based convoys.

By the end of 1943 many U-boats had been recalled to port to be fitted with schnorkel apparatus — basically a breathing tube that allowed a submarine to ventilate its hull and recharge its batteries while at periscope depth. This new 'weapon', by which Dönitz set great store, would allow the U-boats to remain below the surface for much of the time, dramatically reducing their chances of being detected by radar or visual means. It was a long-overdue development. The morale of the crews, many of whom were now inexperienced, was plummeting, and the gnawing fear that an Allied aircraft would suddenly appear kept many of them from pressing home their attacks. Yet despite the loss of a staggering 242 U-boats during the whole of 1943 and the hugely increased naval and air forces now ranged against the survivors, Dönitz still hoped to gain the ascendancy in the New Year, when enough schnorkel-equipped boats would be available for operations in the North Atlantic.

Below left: No fewer than 26 Fleet Air Arm squadrons were assigned to Coastal Command for varying periods during the war. Most were attached to No 16 Group on the South Coast and flew night anti-submarine and anti-shipping patrols in the English Channel. In a typical engagement on 25 March 1943 an Albacore from No 841 Squadron bombed a group of E-boats off Berck-sur-Mer, sinking one. The pilot, Lieutenant S. M. Walsh (left), and his observer, Sub-Lieutenant G. M. Patrick (centre), are seen here at Manston recounting their exploit to Lieutenant J. W. Neale, a veteran of the Swordfish attack on Taranto. **CH 8981**

Below: As the Battle of the Atlantic reached a peak the Air Ministry sought to publicise the sterling efforts of the WAAF in the U-boat war: 'Some thousands of WAAF personnel are serving in Coastal Command. Each may claim her part in the battles of the Atlantic, the Arctic, the North Sea and the Mediterranean. To the aircrews belong the credit of sunken U-boats, lying fathoms deep, and the safe arrival of convoys bringing food to Britain; to the WAAF belongs the satisfaction of making easier the task of the aircrews ...'. This cheerful trio were photographed putting a finishing gloss to a No 210 Squadron Catalina IB (FP259/L) at Pembroke Dock in March 1943. **CH 8974**

Right and below: No 120 Squadron Liberator IIIs undergoing daily inspections at Aldergrove, April 1943. The squadron also had a detachment at Reykjavik to extend its reach into the Atlantic 'Gap'. No 120 had been joined at Aldergrove by No 86 Squadron, now fully operational again after several months spent on crew training. Also, after much prevarication, supplies of new aircraft from the vast American stocks had at last been approved, and 30 new Liberators were assigned to the two squadrons in the spring of 1943, in time for the climactic U-boat battles. **CH 18031, CH 18032**

Above: The smiling crew of this No 120 Squadron Liberator, 'X for X-Ray', was photographed at Aldergrove in the small hours of the morning, prior to taking off on a convoy patrol far out into the Atlantic, April 1943. The unidentified crew comprised captain, second pilot, navigator, flight engineer and two wireless/radar operators, who doubled as gunners. They would not be due back at base until late afternoon. **CH 9587**

Left: Convoy sighted. Despite strong winds and heavy seas 'X for X-Ray' successfully made contact with its designated convoy, after a flight of several hours at low-level to avoid icing conditions in the clouds. For a further three hours the Liberator patrolled out to the front and rear of the convoy, also keeping an eye on stragglers, but there was no sign of any U-boats. After another aircraft arrived on station, 'X for X-Ray' set course for the long trip home, helped by a following wind. It reached Aldergrove after 15 hours in the air. **CH 9602**

Right: No 120 Squadron's detachment at Reykjavik claimed this Type IXC U-boat on 23 April 1943. *U-189* was one of a pair discovered east of Cape Farewell, Greenland, by Flight Lieutenant J. K. Moffatt's crew in Liberator V FL923/V while flying to rendezvous with convoy HX234. Moffatt dropped his six depth charges in two attacks from 50ft, after which the U-boat sank by the stern. **HU 60508E**

Below: After a disastrous start in November 1942, which prompted further training, the North Coates Strike Wing (Nos 143, 236 and 254 Squadrons) finally achieved the success for which it was striving on 18 April 1943, when it attacked a large convoy off the Dutch island of Texel. A 5,000-ton merchant vessel was sunk, and several escort ships damaged. This photograph shows a Beaufighter swooping at mast height over a German M-class minesweeper, having raked its decks with cannon fire. All the RAF aircraft returned safely. **C 3506**

Left: 'Torbeau'. Experiments in 1942 proved that the Beaufighter would make a capable torpedo-bomber. This Mk VI, JL832/A of No 144 Squadron, based at Tain in Scotland, was photographed on 25 April 1943. No 144 Squadron had transferred from Bomber Command in April 1942. It began exchanging its Hampdens for Beaufighters at the beginning of 1943 and flew its first operations with its new aircraft in March. **CH 9755**

Below: Another No 144 Squadron Beaufighter, being fitted with an 18in Mk XV torpedo using a special telescopic cradle designed for the job. The torpedo is fitted with a Mk IV gyro-stabilised MAT (Monoplane Air Tail).
The Beaufighter VI was the fastest torpedo-bomber in the world at this time, a far cry from the Vildebeests available to Coastal Command at the beginning of the war. **CH 9769**

Above: In April 1943 No 144 Squadron joined with No 404 Squadron RCAF to form a second Beaufighter strike wing, based at Wick. The two units flew their first operation together on 27 April, when they attacked a convoy off Norway. One large merchant ship was hit by at least three torpedoes, one of which is seen exploding in this photograph. No Beaufighters were lost. **C 3531**

Above: The North Coates Wing enjoyed further success on the evening of 29 April 1943, when it intercepted another convoy off the Dutch coast. This shot was taken from a No 254 Squadron aircraft during the first minutes of the attack. Two large merchant ships and one of the escorting flak ships were torpedoed and sunk, and several other escorts badly shot up. One Beaufighter from No 143 Squadron failed to return. **C 3524**

Left: May 1943 — 'Black May' — was the worst month of the war for the U-boats; 41 were destroyed, half of them by aircraft. They included *U-266*, caught on the surface in the Bay of Biscay on the 15th by a No 58 Squadron Halifax on its way home from patrol, flown by the CO, Wing Commander Wilfred Oulton. The U-boat can be glimpsed in this shot, bracketed by six depth charges, seconds before it broke apart and sank vertically by the stern. It was a busy time for Oulton and his crew — previously, on 7 May, they had attacked and damaged *U-214* and then had a hand in the destruction of *U-563* on the last day of the month. **C 3575**

Below: A peaceful scene at Castle Archdale (formerly Loch Erne) in Northern Ireland on 20 May 1943, as a seaplane tender passes a Sunderland of No 201 Squadron. Once again the censor has removed all trace of the aircraft's fuselage-mounted ASV aerials. After a lengthy period that saw little action and a number of fatal accidents, No 201 Squadron was rewarded with its first kill on 31 May, when *U-440* was sent to the bottom north-west of Cape Ortegal, on the coast of Spain. A month later *U-518* was bombed and damaged so severely that it was forced to return to port. **CH 11075**

Above: A No 220 Squadron Fortress IIA seen 'bombing up' at Benbecula, in the Outer Hebrides, May 1943. No 220 had recently moved here from Northern Ireland, to operate alongside Coastal Command's other Fortress squadron, No 206. Less well known is No 59 Squadron's brief spell with Boeings at the beginning of the year, flying patrols over the Western Approaches from Chivenor, before converting back to Liberators in April. **CH 11101**

Right: 250lb depth charges are hoisted into the bomb bay of a Fortress at Benbecula. Initially the Boeings could carry a maximum of 14 DCs, but this load was later halved to allow for extra fuel to extend their endurance. Air Ministry 'boffins' had finally developed a shallow-setting firing pistol, thus solving the crucial problem of achieving the correct detonation depth. The Mk XI depth charge, available from the summer of 1942, could be set to explode at an optimum 20ft below the surface, dramatically increasing its effectiveness. **CH 11102**

Above: The presence of aircraft in an otherwise remote location, previously linked to the mainland by boat only, meant that No 220 Squadron flew its share of mercy missions. This patient with acute appendicitis was airlifted to hospital on the mainland in one of the Fortresses, the open waist window serving as a convenient entrance to the aircraft. **CH 11126**

Left: A Fortress radar operator at his set, peering through a light guard at the CRT indicator screen for the tell-tale return from a surfaced U-boat. This shot was posed at base, but in the air alertness was crucial, and operators had to be rotated at regular intervals. From January centimetric radar (ASV Mk III) was in use on some of the Liberator and Wellington squadrons. Crews found its new PPI (Plan Position Indicator) display, which produced a map-like picture of the area covered by the radar beam, more intuitive and easier to interpret than that of earlier versions. Centimetric radar was a major technological leap forward that swung the advantage further in the Allies' favour. **CH 18481**

Right: This No 120 Squadron Liberator crew, led by Flight Lieutenant A. W. Fraser RAAF (centre), was photographed after sinking *U-200* southwest of Iceland on 24 June 1943. Their Liberator I, AM929/H, seen behind, was damaged in the attack and Fraser was forced to return immediately to Reykjavik, completing a difficult landing without incident. Fraser was awarded a Bar to his DFC for his 'magnificent example of determination to destroy the enemy in the face of opposition'. He was killed in a flying accident a year later. The aircraft itself was a veteran of the Atlantic battles and had several other U-boat claims to its credit. It was eventually retired from the front line and transferred to Atlantic ferrying duties with No 231 Squadron but crashed in Canada in April 1945. **C 3767**

Far right: Ten million square miles of sea. The vast extent of Coastal Command's theatre of operations is graphically displayed on this newly commissioned 20ft x 30ft map at Coastal Command Headquarters at Northwood, 9 July 1943. From the Arctic Circle to North Africa, from the coasts of occupied Europe to far out into the Atlantic, the Command's areas of responsibility had expanded to such an extent that the existing situation map had been rendered obsolete. Work on the new map was supervised by Coastal Command's Map Officer, Captain J. H. Adam, Royal Engineers. (The Geographical Section of the General Staff supplied maps for both the RAF and the Army.) **CH 10674**

Above: No 311 (Czech) Squadron celebrated its third anniversary of service with the RAF on 21 July 1943, and an official photographer was on hand to record the event. At the time the squadron had been screened from operations and was in the process of converting to Liberators at Beaulieu. This unnamed crew is seen with Liberator IIIA LV343/12. The Mk IIIA designation had been given to the first batch of 11 Liberator IIIs, delivered from USAAF stocks in the spring of 1942. Subsequent aircraft obtained under Lend-Lease were modified with British equipment. No 311 Squadron's return to anti-submarine operations in August 1943 was marred by the loss of its commanding officer, Wing Commander Jindrich Breitcetl. **CH 18520**

These pages: A victim of the Battle of the Bay was the veteran *U-106*, a Type IXB U-boat responsible for sinking 22 merchant ships. On 2 August 1943 it was set upon by two Sunderlands from Nos 228 and 461 Squadrons, both based at Pembroke Dock. The first two photographs show DV968/M of No 461 Squadron RAAF making its attack run, strafing the U-boat's decks to suppress anti-aircraft fire before releasing its depth charges. In the final photograph in the sequence the submarine is seen sinking by the stern, smoke pouring from its engine compartment. Shell splashes can be seen as the Sunderland gunners keep up their fire. Shortly after this the U-boat blew up, but 36 of her crew of 58 were rescued by the Royal Navy. **HU 81584, HU 81585, C 3881**

Right: A swirling patch of foam and blazing fuel marks the end of a Ju88, shot down by four Beaufighters of No 248 Squadron while on patrol in the Bay of Biscay on 29 July 1943. Barely an hour before, the same Beaufighters had chanced upon an FW200 Condor, and it too had been quickly destroyed. A week later the Luftwaffe exacted revenge when FW190s shot down a No 248 Squadron Beaufighter returning to Predannack after covering an air-sea rescue operation. **C 3685**

Above: On 2 August 1943, Hampden torpedo bombers of No 455 Squadron RAAF attacked a convoy off the Norwegian coast. One aircraft (L4105/D) suffered massive flak damage to its tail — half the elevator was blown away, the starboard fin twisted and the port rudder fouled by debris. The crew were forced to lash a rope around the rudder bar and took turns helping the pilot, Flying Officer Iain Masson, hold the aircraft straight as they limped back to Leuchars for a crash-landing. Not untypically for an 'Australian' squadron this crew actually comprised two Englishmen, a Canadian and a New Zealander! **CH 10730**

Right: Three U-boats were sunk by Coastal Command aircraft on 8 October 1943 around convoy SC143. One of them was *U-643*, depth-charged by two Liberators from No 86 Squadron. This photograph, showing the U-boat stopped and down by the bow, was taken from the third Liberator to arrive on the scene. The stricken submarine eventually blew up and sank, but 18 of her crew survived to be rescued by HMS *Orwell*. It had been a good day for No 86, as earlier another of its aircraft had sunk *U-419*. The third U-boat was claimed by a Sunderland from No 423 Squadron. **C 3933**

Above: Martin (PBM-3B) Mariner I JX103, October 1943. No 524 Squadron was formed at Oban in the same month to evaluate this large flying boat, a small number of which had been supplied to the RAF by the Americans. The squadron worked up on the type between October and December but was then disbanded when it was decided that the RAF would not be adopting the aircraft after all. No 524 was re-formed in May 1944, this time with the tried and tested Wellington XIII. **MH 5097**

Above: The Mosquito was coveted by all RAF Commands, and the first fighter versions to enter service with Coastal Command went to 'B' Flight No 333 (Norwegian) Squadron (formerly No 1477 Flight) in the spring of 1943. The Norwegians had been flying reconnaissance missions and clandestine operations over their home country using Catalinas, but with the Mosquito they were far less vulnerable to interception. These Mosquito IIs were photographed at their base at Leuchars in October 1943. **HU 90816**

Right: Liberator V BZ877, serving with No 86 Squadron at Ballykelly, displaying the standard Coastal Command grey and white 'herring gull' camouflage, November 1943. The Liberator V, available from the spring of 1943, had an operational endurance of about 15 hours with a 1,500lb offensive load. It was fitted with centimetric radar, either in a 'chin' radome or more usually in a retractable 'dustbin' unit in the ventral fuselage (in the space occupied by the ball turret in bomber versions). A wing-mounted Leigh Light and even rocket projectiles could also be carried, although these items came at the expense of fuel or ammunition. Some aircraft had their top turrets removed as a weight-saving measure. **CH 11800**

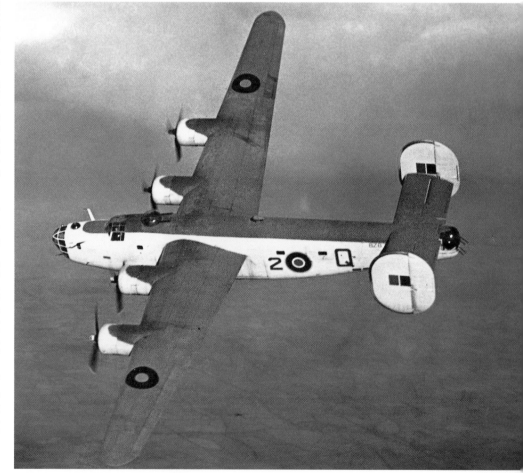

Above: Liberator V BZ791 at Boscombe Down in November 1943. This aircraft was used by the A&AEE for test purposes and was never assigned to an operational squadron. By the end of 1943 there were just over 100 Liberators in Coastal Command service, though well under a half were actually available for operations. In addition three US Navy PB4Y-1 Liberator squadrons, with a total of 35 aircraft, had been seconded to No 19 Group for anti-submarine operations over the Bay. Ironically the Battle of the Atlantic was won without the benefit of the extra Liberators now finally entering service, yet numbers were never quite sufficient to re-equip Coastal Command's Wellington squadrons as originally intended. **ATP 11552B**

Above: On 23 November 1943 a force of 23 Beaufighters from Nos 236 and 254 Squadrons, escorted by Spitfires, attacked a southbound convoy off Texel on the Dutch coast. This dramatic shot was taken as the first of two torpedoes slammed into the largest ship in the convoy, a 7,000-ton tanker, breaking its back. Barrage balloons can be seen in the background. Several escorting vessels were set on fire during strafing attacks, but the flak was intense, and four Beaufighters were shot down. The formation leader, Squadron Leader H. Shannon, was hit and severely wounded but managed to bring his aircraft home. **C 3939**

Above: A Fortress IIA taking off from Lagens, on the island of Terceira in the Azores, November 1943. Nos 206 and 220 Squadrons had recently moved in to conduct Atlantic patrols and protect convoys heading to Gibraltar and the Mediterranean. On 9 November a No 220 Squadron crew, commanded by Flight Lieutenant Roderick Drummond, claimed the first kill by an Azores-based aircraft when they sank *U-707*. No 206 Squadron moved back to the UK in March 1944, but No 220 stayed here for the duration of the war. **CA 9**

Above: Detachments of Leigh Light Wellington XIVs from Nos 172 and 179 Squadrons were based in the Azores between November 1943 and April 1944. This aircraft being refuelled at Lagens bears on its fuselage the number '1', which was the identifier for No 172 Squadron at the time. During this period of the war Coastal Command aircraft often lacked squadron codes, and when several squadrons were based at the same airfield a single number was allocated to each unit for identification purposes. The scheme caused much confusion, however, and standard two-letter squadron codes were later reinstated. **CA 143**

Above: Beaufighter X LZ440 of No 254 Squadron, December 1943. In service since June, the Mk X was fitted with Hercules XVII engines, tuned for peak power at low level. As well as its internal armament of four 20mm cannon and a .303in machine gun in the rear compartment for self-defence, it could carry one 18in torpedo, eight rocket projectiles or 2,500lb of bombs. At this time Coastal Command's Beaufighter squadrons were located at North Coates (Nos 236 and 254), Wick (Nos 144 and 404 RCAF), Portreath (Nos 143 and 235) and Leuchars (Nos 455 RAAF and 489 RNZAF). No 248 Squadron was in the process of converting to Mosquitos at Predannack. **CH 18579**

Left: A German 'blockade runner' burning fiercely in the Bay of Biscay, after being attacked by a No 311 Squadron Liberator, 27 December 1943. Such ships carried cargoes of essential war materials, including rubber, chemicals and high-grade metal ores from Japan and the Far East, but their numbers decreased as the war progressed and Allied aircraft came to dominate the waters around the enemy coast. As standard depth charges were of little use against ships, new dual-purpose 600lb anti-submarine bombs had been developed for Coastal Command, suitable for attacks against targets above or below the waves. They could be dropped from low level or from as high as 5,000ft using the new Mark XIV bomb-sight. **C 4002**

1944

> *'The Strike Wing policy was fully justified when large convoys were the target, and the 'Rover' patrols, single aircraft or in pairs, using bad weather to effect surprise, took a steady toll of Germany's wasting merchant fleet.'*
>
> (Air Chief Marshal Sir Philip Joubert de la Ferté, *Birds and Fishes — The Story of Coastal Command*)

At the beginning of the year there was yet another change at the top of Coastal Command, with Air Chief Marshal Sir Sholto Douglas taking over on 20 January 1944. His Command had grown into a powerful force, its main anti-submarine component comprising seven Liberator and seven Sunderland squadrons, five Wellington squadrons and two each of Halifaxes, Fortresses and Catalinas. Three more Liberator squadrons were on loan from the US Navy. Two Hudson squadrons were still operating in the anti-submarine role, from Gibraltar and the Azores. For anti-shipping duties there were now eight Beaufighter units, and two squadrons were equipped with the Mosquito. In total over 600 aircraft were on strength, although fewer than half of these were available for operations.

Sholto Douglas's principal opponent, Grossadmiral Karl Dönitz, had by now been appointed head of the entire German Navy but retained operational control of the U-boat arm. The force at his disposal was still formidable, but hopes now rested on new equipment, such as the schnorkel, and ultimately on the entry into service of advanced new U-boats, to offset the preponderance of Allied ships and aircraft. On 2 January *U-539* slipped out of Lorient, the first schnorkel-equipped U-boat to embark on an operational patrol. A month later a second boat, *U-264*, set out. By June 1944 at least 35 U-boats had been fitted with schnorkels.

Given the opportunity, U-boats still attempted to steal through the Straits of Gibraltar and into the Mediterranean, where Allied shipping was less well protected. In one incident on 24 February a No 202 Squadron Catalina joined US Navy aircraft and surface units in damaging *U-761*, later scuttled by its crew. However, the progress of the war meant that Gibraltar was becoming less important strategically, and Coastal Command's anti-submarine squadrons there were gradually removed. By June only No 202 remained, Nos 179 and 233 having been transferred to the Azores.

In the first three months of 1944 some 60 U-boats were destroyed, the vast majority in the Atlantic. Coastal Command was responsible, wholly or in part, for 11 of these kills. During the same period only 54 Allied merchant ships were sunk. Once again Dönitz's attempts to reinstitute wolf-pack tactics had failed, and the U-boats were ordered instead to operate singly. This change in tactics made them less effective but also harder

to find. Coastal Command's only U-boat kill for April was scored by the Canadians of No 162 Squadron on the 17th, when they sank *U-342* off Iceland.

By the spring of 1944 there were fewer U-boats at sea, as many were being re-equipped in French ports in readiness for the invasion which all knew was coming. Dönitz received instructions to conserve his force and assemble the bulk of it in the Biscay ports in readiness for the Allied assault on France. U-boats in Norway made the perilous trip on the surface through the narrows between Scotland and Iceland, the northern transit route, patrolled by Nos 15 and 18 Groups of Coastal Command. In May five U-boats were sunk off Norway and the Faeroes, with Nos 59 and 210 Squadrons bagging two apiece.

For many months now preparations for the invasion of France had dominated Allied operations. The exact location and timing of the assault on Europe was, of course, a closely-guarded secret, but the German High Command knew only too well that at some point in the spring or summer of 1944 they could expect a major assault to be launched against a section of the northern French coast. The Allied plan necessarily involved a huge amount of shipping, and, while the Luftwaffe could easily be contained, there was more concern in the Allied camp over the danger posed by U-boats in the congested waters of the English Channel.

Allied naval planners anticipated up to 200 U-boats being available to counter the invasion, and Coastal Command was given the vital task of protecting the assault and support forces from their predations. In April ACM Sir Sholto Douglas issued instructions to his Command. No 16 Group would look after the eastern end of the English Channel and the North Sea, while No 19 Group was given the much larger task of blocking the wider and more vulnerable Western Approaches. Meanwhile Nos 15 and 18 Groups would continue to cover the Atlantic convoys and the northern transit route.

Coastal Command's order of battle was formidable and included various Fleet Air Arm squadrons on temporary attachment. No 19 Group was by far the strongest component,

Above rght: U-426 had the dubious distinction of becoming Coastal Command's first kill of 1944. The Type VIIC U-boat was spotted on 8 January in the Bay of Biscay west of Nantes by a Sunderland of No 10 Squadron RAAF, flown by Flying Officer J. P. Roberts. It is seen here sinking by the stern after being straddled by six depth charges and under fire from the Sunderland's turrets. The crew of 51 all perished. **C 4801**

Right: The Mosquito XVIII, the so-called 'Tsetse', was armed with a 6pdr (57mm) Molins gun for use against surfaced U-boats. This aircraft, MM424, seen in February 1944, was one of only 17 production versions built. The barrel of the Molins gun, which was loaded automatically, can be seen protruding from the underside of the nose. The first 'Tsetses' were delivered to No 248 Squadron's Mosquito Conversion Flight in October 1943, and flew sorties over the Bay of Biscay, attacking shipping and U-boats. On 25 March 1944 U-976 was sunk near St Nazaire, and U-960 damaged off La Pallice two days later. **ATP 12595B**

comprising 24 anti-submarine squadrons, including Nos 179 and 206 brought back from Gibraltar and the Azores. The group would operate in 12 pre-defined areas stretching between southern Ireland and the Loire, flying continuous patrols so as to deny the U-boats access, or at least force them to dive prematurely and exhaust their batteries. Appropriately enough it was named Operation 'Cork'. No 16 Group's role was in many ways a secondary one, as the U-boats were not expected to attempt to traverse the heavily-mined Straits of Dover. Its prime function was to guard against E-boat attack.

If April and May had been relatively quiet, June was to see a flurry of activity as the invasion of France finally got underway on the 6th. As expected, the U-boats set out from Brest and the Biscay ports, their target the mass of shipping now off the Normandy coast. The majority were not yet fitted with schnorkel devices and were forced to journey on the surface under the illusory cover of darkness. The Leigh Light-equipped Wellingtons, Liberators and Sunderlands of Coastal Command were waiting for them. Between 7 and 13 June six U-boats were sent to the bottom in the Bay and the Channel approaches. A handful of schnorkel boats did succeed in penetrating the Allied screen, sinking a number of escorts and landing ships, but were soon driven out into less-congested waters.

Other U-boats were attacked off Norway and north of Scotland as they made their lengthy journeys to reach the invasion area. One squadron enjoying a spell of success in these parts was Wick-based No 162 Squadron, RCAF, operating Cansos (Canadian-built PBY-5s). The squadron had been transferred from the Royal Canadian Air Force to Coastal Command at the beginning of the year. It sank four U-boats and shared in the destruction of a fifth, but not without tragic loss. On 24 June Flight Lieutenant David Hornell sighted a surfaced U-boat off the Faeroes and immediately attacked. Although his Canso was hit several times and set ablaze by return fire, Hornell continued his attack, successfully straddling the U-boat with depth charges. With the submarine gone, Hornell put his blazing aircraft down on the choppy water and the crew took to the single available life-raft. Three of them, including Hornell, died of exposure before they could be rescued. Flight Lieutenant Hornell became the only RCAF airman in Coastal Command to be awarded the Victoria Cross.

In all, Coastal Command sank 14 U-boats and damaged two more in June. Another six were destroyed in July, four off Norway

Above left: Fitters working on the 1,200hp Pratt & Whitney R-1830 Twin Wasps of a No 224 Squadron Liberator at St Eval, 26 February 1944. The Cornish airfield was home to Nos 53, 224 and 547 Squadrons, all flying Leigh Light-equipped Mk Vs on patrols over the Bay of Biscay and the Western Approaches. Coastal Command's other Liberator squadrons were at Predannack (No 311), Ballykelly (Nos 59 and 120) and Reykjavik (No 86). Three US Navy PB4Y squadrons were located at Dunkeswell. **CH 12371**

Left: Ready for the off. Wing Commander R. T. F. Gates (far left), CO of No 53 Squadron, chats to the 10-man crew of Liberator V 'H for Harry', about to set off on an anti-submarine patrol from St Eval, 26 February 1944. Large crews were characteristic of daylight anti-submarine operations — the extra WOp/AGs allowed for frequent rotation of radar and visual watches, thus maintaining alertness. Note the Boulton Paul rear turret, fitted to most Liberators in RAF service. **CH 12366**

and two in the Bay. That month another Coastal Command VC was awarded, this time to Flying Officer John Alexander Cruickshank, a Catalina pilot with No 210 Squadron, based at Sullom Voe. On 17 July Cruickshank caught *U-347* on the surface off northern Norway, but in the ensuing attack his depth charges hung up. Forced to make a second run-in, his aircraft was hit repeatedly by accurate return fire from the U-boat, and the navigator/bomb-aimer was killed. Though badly wounded, Cruickshank executed a perfect second attack, and the U-boat was blown apart. During the five-hour return trip Cruickshank lapsed in and out of consciousness and refused morphia so that he could help his inexperienced co-pilot bring the aircraft home to a safe landing. Happily, he recovered from a total of 72 individual wounds!

In August the advance of American troops towards the French Atlantic ports prompted a general evacuation of the U-boats to Norway, via the west coast of Ireland and around the north of Scotland. Coastal Command aircraft were involved in the sinking of five more U-boats off the French coast, including *U-981*, sent to the bottom after running into a minefield and then being depth-charged by a Halifax of No 502 Squadron. By September the U-boats had gone from the French ports, and a major chapter in Coastal Command's war had closed.

Coastal Command's anti-shipping campaign also stepped up a gear during 1944 as a plentiful supply of crews and aircraft finally became available. In February the North Coates Wing had been brought back up to strength with the return of No 143 Squadron, previously detached for operations over the Bay, and it continued to mount successful operations against convoys off the Netherlands and Germany's North Sea coast. With enemy shipping now usually moving under the cover of darkness, the wing tried attacking at night, illuminated by flares dropped from No 415 Squadron Wellingtons. These operations (codenamed 'Gilbeys') were difficult to stage effectively, but No 254 Squadron managed to sink a freighter off Borkum on the night of 5/6 March. The Wick Wing (Nos 144 and 404 Squadrons) was also now in business, employing the new rocket projectiles against vessels off the Norwegian coast with devastating effect. A third Beaufighter strike wing, comprising No 455 Squadron RAAF and No 489 Squadron RNZAF (both newly converted from Hampdens), was activated in March and based at Leuchars. It too hunted off Norway.

Much of Coastal Command's anti-shipping strength was deployed south in the run-up to Operation 'Overlord', although not all squadrons were actually used on D-Day itself. In May No 143 moved to Manston in Kent, Nos 144 and 404 Squadrons went to Davidstow Moor in Cornwall, and Nos 455 and 489 Squadrons relocated to Langham on the Norfolk coast. E-boats and other small naval vessels were a favoured target, but merchant shipping and submarines were also attacked. No 415 Squadron RCAF, another unit previously equipped with Hampdens, continued to fly specialised night operations against E-boats and other vessels, using its peculiar combination of Leigh Light-fitted Wellingtons and Fairey Albacores, the one to spot and the other to attack. It was also called upon to lay smokescreens and spot the fall of naval gunfire against targets ashore. Another feature of the period was the temporary transfer of several Fleet Air Arm Swordfish and Avenger squadrons to Coastal Command control, operating at both ends of the English Channel. They too played their part in protecting the huge Allied invasion forces from surface and underwater threats during that momentous summer.

The Mosquito had been in operational service with No 248 Squadron since March, principally employed over the Bay of Biscay on fighter-reconnaissance and anti-shipping missions. Most were standard Mk VI fighter-bombers, but the squadron also had a small number of Mk XIII 'Tsetses', armed with a 57mm gun able to punch a hole in the side of any ship or U-boat. In June they were joined at Portreath in Cornwall by

No 235 Squadron, now also re-equipped with the Mosquito VI. The two squadrons contributed most effectively to the continuing blockade of the Biscay ports.

With the Allies firmly established in France, the Beaufighter units began returning to their airfields in eastern England, although for a time detachments from No 236 and 404 Squadrons were recalled to the West Country, operating with the Portreath Mosquito Wing. The aircraft ranged south along the coast of western France in a concerted effort to sink what was left of the Kriegsmarine's surface ships in this area, most of which were bottled up in ports now besieged by the advancing Allies. Flak ships, minesweepers, torpedo boats and other small naval craft were systematically blitzed by cannon and rocket fire. No fewer than 29 ships were sunk in August, and by the end of September there were few targets left. Further east, enemy traffic along the Dutch and German North Sea coasts had slowed to an inconsequential trickle after receiving similar attention (No 16 Group sank 26 vessels in July and August). As a consequence the anti-shipping squadrons were again redeployed, most going back to Scotland for operations across the North Sea to Norway.

By late October four squadrons of Beaufighters (Nos 144, 404, 455 and 489) had moved to Dallachy in Aberdeenshire,

Below: A stick of six depth charges from Sunderland III EK591 'U-Uncle' of No 422 Squadron RCAF splashes into the sea alongside *U-625*, caught shadowing a convoy 400 miles west of Ireland on 10 March 1944. Seconds later they detonated, inflicting massive damage to the submarine's aft compartments. Unable to dive, the U-boat circled for over an hour and a half — during which the Sunderland crew kept watch, observing some of the crew taking to the water — before it eventually sank by the stern. The attack was carried out by Flight Lieutenant Sid Butler, who was screening a new crew on their first operational sortie. It was the squadron's first — and last — U-boat kill of the war. **C 4286**

Above: Wellington XIV MP818 at Boscombe Down, April 1944. This, the latest Coastal Command variant of the venerable 'Wimpy', was fitted with ASV Mk III radar in a 'chin' radome, a radio altimeter for accurate low-level flying and a retractable Leigh Light aft of the bomb bay. The normal offensive load consisted of six 250lb depth charges, the rest of the bomb bay being occupied by overload fuel tanks, which enabled the aircraft to fly sorties of 10 or 11 hours' duration. A .303in Browning machine-gun could be carried in the nose for flak suppression. **ATP 11731C**

while three Mosquito units (Nos 235, 248 and the recently-converted No 143) were concentrated at nearby Banff. The Norwegians of No 333 Squadron brought their Mosquitos to Banff too, to operate in the 'pathfinder' role over their homeland. Nos 236 and 254 Squadrons remained where they were at North Coates. Thus placed, Coastal Command's formidable anti-shipping force embarked on its final and most successful period of operations.

The volume of seaborne traffic between Germany and Norway increased steadily in the last months of 1944. In addition to the normal imports of iron ore and other raw materials, the new U-boat bases in Norway had to be supplied, and German troops were being gradually withdrawn from the far north of the country and from Finland too. With its anti-shipping operations winding down elsewhere, the RAF was free to intensify its offensive campaign in Norwegian waters. But Coastal Command operations off the coast of Norway were made more problematic by the fact that enemy vessels had taken to laying up in the precipitous fjords during the day, only venturing out at night or in adverse weather. Regular reconnaissance patrols were flown in an effort to catch the ships in open waters, and a number of pre-dawn attacks were carried out with the aid of marker flares laid off the coast by ASR Warwicks, but it was clear that the RAF squadrons would have to go into the fjords themselves. Of invaluable assistance were 'outrider' aircraft, usually crewed by Norwegians with local

knowledge, flying ahead of the main attack force to sniff out potential targets. In a successful operation on 8 November the Dallachy Wing was led into the perilously narrow Midtgulen Fjord and sank two coasters moored alongside its steep walls.

On 13 November squadrons from the Banff and Dallachy Wings flew their first operation together, penetrating Rekefjord, where they damaged one merchant vessel and sank an escort. But sorties were not always productive, the weather providing the biggest obstacle to efficient searches. On 21 November a large strike force of 32 Mosquitos and 42 Beaufighters was despatched on a patrol off Alesund but failed to find any suitable targets to attack and had to abort due to poor visibility. A resurgence of the Luftwaffe posed another hazard to the strike wings, especially as only one Fighter Command Mustang squadron was available for escort duties. On 7 December two Mosquitos and a Beaufighter were lost after a large force of enemy fighters pounced during another operation off Alesund.

Further south the congested waters between Norway, Denmark and Sweden, namely the Kattegat and Skagerrak, had become another focus of anti-shipping activity, this time involving the Halifaxes of Nos 58 and 502 Squadrons. Operating singly under the cover of darkness, they used ASV radar to locate supply boats steaming between Norway and the Baltic ports, dropping flares to illuminate their targets before delivering attacks with sticks of 500lb bombs from 5,000ft. When conditions were unsuitable for shipping searches here the Halifaxes flew bombing raids against vessels anchored in Norwegian ports further north.

Norway had become the new base of operations for the U-boats. In the autumn of 1944 Dönitz ordered them to concentrate their activities around the west coast of Britain. There were rich pickings to be had in the congested waterways of the Irish Sea and the Bristol Channel for those U-boat skippers skilful and daring enough to operate under the very noses of the enemy. As might be expected, schnorkel-equipped U-boats proved much harder to locate and sink. As ACM Sir Philip Joubert later wrote, 'What bothered the aircrews was that, in lieu of a fully surfaced U-boat, or even a periscope, all that they now could see was a wake and a small cloud of steam, as the schnorkelling U-boat went its way.'

In November Sholto Douglas ordered the reintroduction of close air support for inbound convoys. No 15 Group was reinforced, its aircraft flying box patrols ahead and to the flanks of the ships as they approached British waters. In the last four months of the year only five U-boats were sunk by Coastal Command. It was fortunate indeed that by this stage of the war

the overall number of operational U-boats was so low, and the weight of Allied countermeasures so great, that the best they could achieve was the sinking of a mere handful of ships.

The year closed for Coastal Command as it did for the Allies in general. Despite confidence in their overwhelming material superiority, there was consternation that the war was dragging into a sixth year without the collapse that so many had thought inevitable. On land and at sea the Germans had found the strength for renewed resistance. Schnorkel-equipped U-boats posed a serious threat to the mass of Allied shipping, and the first examples of a completely new and far superior class of submarine were known to be nearing operational readiness. Though there was no doubt over the final outcome, there was still work to be done.

Left and this page: This sequence was taken from a Canso (a Canadian-built Catalina) of No 162 Squadron RCAF during a successful attack on *U-342*, southwest of Iceland on 17 April 1944. One of the depth charges can be seen 'porpoising' out of the water. After 18 months of uneventful duty on Canada's east coast, No 162 'Osprey' Squadron was loaned to Coastal Command in January 1944, based initially at Reykjavik and then Wick. It became the RCAF's most successful anti-submarine squadron, sinking five U-boats single-handedly, of which *U-342* was the first. **HU 81252, HU 81253, HU 81254**

Above: Wellington XIV HF385 of No 612 Squadron, under tow at Chivenor, April 1944. The WAAF tractor driver is 20-year-old LACW Felicity Lambert. Four of Coastal Command's five Wellington XIV squadrons (Nos 172, 304, 407 and 612) had been brought together at this Devon airfield in the run-up to D-Day for anti-submarine operations over the western end of the Channel, most of which were flown at night. The fifth, No 179 Squadron, had just returned from the Azores to Predannack to operate over the Bay of Biscay. **CH 12719**

Right: A heavily armed escort vessel seen from below mast height during a convoy attack by the North Coates Wing off the Frisian Islands, 20 April 1944. The Ministry caption writer recorded drily: 'It will be noted that while gun positions and guns are showing, the gun crews have been driven from their posts by the terrific weight of fire of the Beaufighters.' One enemy ship was torpedoed, two escorts left ablaze and a third seriously damaged, at a cost of one Beaufighter that failed to return. **C 4314**

Above: Sunderland ML839/A of No 10 Squadron RAAF, May 1944. This aircraft, originally built as a Centaurus-powered Mk III, had been fitted experimentally with Pratt & Whitney Twin Wasps, on the initiative of the station commander at Mount Batten. The Sunderland had always been underpowered, and having to run its engines at full power for much of the time greatly reduced its service life. The Twin Wasps provided the extra horsepower needed. Shorts itself had thought of the same idea, producing its own prototype. The result was the Sunderland V, the first version able to maintain height on only two engines. **CH 21574**

Left: Another view of Sunderland ML839 during tests in May 1944. ASV aerials are clearly visible, but later Mk IIIs and all Mk Vs were fitted with centimetric radar, the scanners neatly enclosed in streamlined radomes below the outer wing panels. Note too how the aircraft's top surfaces are faded and weathered from months of duty over the Atlantic. This Sunderland was eventually lost on 12 October 1944, when it sank at its moorings in a gale. **CH 21577**

Right: The only crew in Coastal Command to sink two U-boats in one sortie was that of Flying Officer Kenneth Owen Moore, a Canadian serving with No 224 Squadron. 'Kayo' Moore, seen here on the right with his bomb aimer Warrant Officer Johnston 'Jock' McDowell, achieved this dramatic feat on the night of 7/8 June 1944, when flying a 'Cork' patrol over the western end of the Channel. In clear moonlit conditions (which meant the Leigh Light was not required) the Liberator crew came across *U-373* making its way towards the invasion area. Moore achieved a perfect straddle with six depth charges and blew the U-boat apart. Barely 20 minutes later his radar operator detected another surfaced U-boat. This time the target was *U-Flak 1* (formerly *U-441*), a converted 'flak' U-boat fitted with additional gun platforms. Moore flew through its heavy return fire, dropped his remaining depth charges accurately and sent the U-boat to the bottom. **CH 20902**

Below: Flying Officer 'Kayo' Moore's crew in front of their Liberator V at St Eval, June 1944. From left are Flying Officer A. P. Gibb (navigator), Flying Officer J. M. Ketcheson (2nd Pilot) and Warrant Officers E. E. Davison, W. P. Foster, D. H. Greise and W. N. Werbeski (all WOp/AGs). Not present are Flight Sergeant I. Webb (rear gunner) and Sergeant J Hamer (flight engineer). WO Davison is holding the most important member of the crew, a toy panda by the name of Warrant Officer 'Dinty' DFM! **CH 13725**

Above: Little friends. A Sunderland and its Spitfire escort passing the Eddystone Lighthouse, 14 miles south of Plymouth, June/July 1944. Six of Coastal Command's seven home-based Sunderland squadrons were involved in the huge effort to protect the flanks of the invasion, flying continuous anti-submarine operations in the Bay of Biscay, and over the western end of the English Channel as part of Operation 'Cork'. On 7 June Nos 201 and 228 Squadrons each sank a U-boat in the Bay of Biscay. Attacks by Luftwaffe aircraft were now becoming rare, but crews were still grateful for the protection offered by the Allied fighter umbrella. **CH 13485**

Left: Liberator VI EV882 of No 206 Squadron, June/July 1944. The Liberator VI and the virtually identical Mk VIII were based on the B-24H and J models and were the last variants used by Coastal Command. Their most obvious distinguishing feature was the addition of a nose turret — a development prompted by American losses sustained in head-on fighter attacks on raids over Europe. Deliveries of the Mk VI began at the beginning of 1944, and by D-Day it was in service with Nos 53 and 206 Squadrons, followed by Nos 224 and 547 later in the year. The Mk VIII had improved radar and entered RAF service in the summer of 1944. In this view the aircraft's retracted ASV radome is visible, protruding slightly below the ventral fuselage. **CH 20692**

Above and below: After the Allied armies had become established in Normandy and the naval threat to the invasion forces had receded, the Beaufighter squadrons were once again concentrated in eastern England for North Sea attacks. No 143 Squadron rejoined Nos 236 and 254 at North Coates, while Nos 144 and 404 RCAF Squadrons moved to Strubby in Lincolnshire. These two photographs were taken during a combined attack carried out by both wings on a convoy off Heligoland on 8 July 1944. Thirty-nine Beaufighters were involved, one of which can be seen low over the water having just dropped its torpedo. Three freighters and a minesweeper were sunk during the strike. **HU 81249, HU 81250**

Above: Ground crew re-arm a No 489 Squadron 'Torbeau' at Langham in Norfolk, June/July 1944. This RNZAF squadron usually flew alongside neighbouring No 455 Squadron RAAF on anti-shipping strikes, the latter acting in the anti-flak role. During the invasion period operations against E-boats and other small craft off the French coast became an important activity, for which the Beaufighters carried 250lb or 500lb bombs. **HU 81248**

Above: The Langham Strike Wing was in action on 15 July 1944, when 34 Beaufighters from Nos 455 and 489 Squadrons, operating with No 144 from Strubby, surprised a convoy off the southern coast of Norway. Wing Commander Jack Davenport of No 455 Squadron, leading the strike, later reported: 'I have seen some fires burning, but not like the three that were going when we had broken off our attack. Then one merchantman blew up, throwing black smoke up to 500ft. When the smoke had settled, there was nothing to be seen of the ship. I have never seen a convoy blitzed like this one.' Two other merchant ships were left blazing, and several of the escorts were also set on fire or damaged. All the Beaufighters returned safely. **C 4469**

Above: Rocket-armed Swordfish IIs of No 816 Squadron, Fleet Air Arm, based at Perranporth and St Merryn, July 1944. The aircraft are wearing the AEAF (Allied Expeditionary Air Force) identification markings, or 'invasion stripes', specified for Operation 'Overlord'. The Fleet Air Arm was no stranger to co-operating with the RAF, and in the spring of 1944 three Swordfish and three Avenger squadrons were transferred to Coastal Command control, primarily for night anti-E-boat sorties at either end of the English Channel. No 816 was disbanded in August, but several FAA squadrons remained on loan throughout the autumn. **A 24983**

Above: In July and August 1944 Mosquitos of No 248 Squadron and No 235 (newly converted from Beaufighters) were operating together on escort and anti-shipping strikes along the west coast of France. Among their targets were Dornier Do217s preying on Allied ships with remote-controlled HS 293 glider bombs. On the evening of 9 August a dozen Mosquito VIs from No 235 Squadron and a pair of Mk XVIII 'Tsetses' from No 248 encountered four of these aircraft over the Gironde estuary. The photograph shows a Mosquito orbiting the funeral pyre of one of two Dorniers destroyed in this distinctly one-sided engagement. **C 4550**

Above: The operations room at Coastal Command headquarters at Northwood. In this photograph, released in August 1944, WAAF plotters and 'special duties clerks' record the details of convoy movements and alter the positions of ships, aircraft and submarines. The tapes on the map indicate the various numbered patrol areas covered by RAF aircraft (note the intensive coverage of the Bay of Biscay). One airwoman wears a special safety harness, designed to lower her gently to the floor should she slip off the ladder! **CH 13663**

Above left: On 12 August 1944 the *Sauerland*, a heavily armed *Sperrbrecher* (mine-detector ship), was hit off La Pallice by Beaufighters of No 236 Squadron and a detachment from No 404 Squadron RCAF, both operating from Davidstow Moor. The ship was left floundering and later was finished off by the Royal Navy. The aircraft flying overhead in this photograph is reportedly that of Wing Commander Ken Gatward, the CO of No 404 Squadron and one of the RAF's leading anti-shipping 'aces'. Two more *Sperrbrecher*, the *Magdeburg* and the *Schwanheim*, were sunk the next day by the same squadrons. Such was Coastal Command's thoroughness that by the end of August there was virtually nothing left to sink off the coast of western France. **C 4546**

Above: Sunderland EK573/P of No 10 Squadron RAAF 'unsticks' after picking up three survivors from a Wellington shot down in the Bay of Biscay, 27 August 1944. Despite a heavy swell — and the knowledge that many such landing attempts had ended in disaster — Flight Lieutenant W. B. (Bill) Tilley executed a successful rescue. The No 172 Squadron Wellington had crashed after being hit by return fire during an attack on *U-534* the previous night. The episode revealed another act of heroism. A fourth man, Flying Officer Roderick Gray RCAF, had also escaped from the Wellington. Although wounded he had insisted on others' being given space in the only available dinghy and clung on to the side instead. He succumbed during the night, and for his courage and selflessness he was posthumously awarded the George Cross. **C 4614**

Left: The Norwegian-registered D/S *Ursa* manœuvres desperately to avoid rocket and cannon fire from aircraft of the Banff Strike Wing, 19 September 1944. Three steamships — *Ursa*, *Lynx* and *Tyrifjord* — were making their way from Hamburg to Tromso and Hammerfest when attacked by 21 Beaufighters and 11 Mosquitos in a fjord near Stavenes. *Ursa* suffered damage but survived, while the other two vessels were sunk. A Beaufighter of No 144 Squadron was shot down. **C 4835**

Above left: Death of a ship. A mushroom cloud of oily black smoke marks the destruction of the Norwegian 1,202-ton tanker *Inger Johanne*, set ablaze by a combined strike force of 21 Beaufighters and 17 Mosquitos from the Banff and Dallachy Wings off Lillesand on 15 October 1944. Two rocket-armed Beaufighters roar overhead as another salvo scores a direct hit. The 16 Norwegian seamen on board were all killed. **C 4943**

Left: Pulverised. The *Inger Johanne*'s single escorting flak ship, Vp1605 *Mosel*, offered scant protection and was itself soon engulfed in a torrent of fire. In this dramatic photograph the sea boils around the stricken vessel as a No 404 Squadron aircraft, still wearing 'invasion stripes', passes overhead at mast height. The ship eventually blew up and sank. There were no casualties among the RAF aircraft. **C 4944**

Top: The Vickers Warwick was a development of the Wellington but was never used in its intended bombing role. Left behind by more modern designs, the Mk I was chosen instead for air-sea rescue duties within Coastal Command, in which capacity it entered service in October 1943. The Mk II was used for training and meteorological duties. Then came the Warwick GR V, the only version used by the RAF for front-line duties, which entered service with No 179 Squadron at St Eval in November 1944 (replacing the unit's Wellington XIVs). This view of PN698 on test with the A&AEE shows the ASV radome mounted below the cockpit and the retracted Leigh Light in the rear fuselage. **HU 81251**

Above: Mosquito VI HX918 was delivered to the A&AEE at Boscombe Down in November 1943 for rocket-projectile (RP) tests. This photograph of the aircraft was released in December 1944, by which time the Mosquito crews of the Banff Strike Wing (Nos 235, 248 and newly-converted 143 Squadrons) had completed training with the weapon and were using it to great effect against enemy shipping in Norwegian waters. The Wing's first operational RP sortie was flown on 26 October. With rockets established as the main strike weapon, production of the now redundant Mk XVIII 'Tsetse' was quickly terminated. **CH 14288**

1945

'The enemy's new U-boat tactics had resulted in a serious reduction in sightings and attacks, while on the other hand in January 1945 no less than twenty-two of our merchant ships were sunk. Ten of these sinkings took place in the Irish Sea and the South-Western Approaches, something grimly reminiscent of the early days of the war.'

(Air Chief Marshal Sir Philip Joubert de la Ferté, *Birds and Fishes — The Story of Coastal Command*)

In the final year of the war Coastal Command's main tasks remained the same, but the geographical focus of its activity had changed. The land war had shifted eastwards, and German naval strength was restricted largely to the Baltic ports and Norway. Since the invasion of Europe in the summer of 1944 Coastal Command's main anti-submarine effort had switched from the Atlantic and the Western Approaches to the waters around the United Kingdom, where the U-boats were now concentrating their activities, and with some success. There was no let-up in the anti-shipping war either. Merchant traffic along the North Sea coast of the Netherlands and Germany had been effectively disrupted, but valuable convoys continued to hug the Norwegian coastline and offered rich pickings for the strike wings based in Scotland.

At the beginning of 1945 Coastal Command had almost 750 front-line aircraft, of which just over 400 were available for operations. No 15 Group had seven squadrons for Atlantic operations, all but one based in Northern Ireland. No 16 Group in the south and east had five, including the North Coates Wing, plus another three Swordfish squadrons on loan from the Fleet Air Arm. No 19 Group in the South West was, as ever, well equipped, with eight RAF squadrons, mostly Wellingtons and Sunderlands, and four US Navy PB4Y units. More powerful still was No 18 Group, comprising 17 squadrons. They included the Banff and Dallachy Strike Wings and, reflecting the change in strategic emphasis, a sizeable anti-submarine force of Liberators, Halifaxes and Catalinas to cover the U-boat transit routes from Norway and the Baltic.

Dönitz still had 144 operational U-boats under his command, with many more working up or training. They had become much better at evading Allied aircraft and surface forces, their schnorkels enabling them to run their diesel engines and recharge their batteries while submerged. For Coastal Command the relative dearth of sightings and sinkings characteristic of the last months of 1944 continued into the New Year. No U-boats were sunk in January, and the only success in February was the sinking of *U-927* in the Channel by a Warwick of No 179 Squadron.

The Admiralty was forced to increase defensive measures for Allied shipping in the waters around Britain and requested that more US Navy units be transferred to Coastal Command. The convoys now moved with an unprecedented level of air and naval protection, which by and large was successful in discouraging U-boat attacks, but the lack of confirmed kills was worrying. In an effort to remedy the situation, offensive day and night patrols over the northern transit areas and the Norwegian coastline were stepped up. And not all the U-boats were making their way towards British coastal waters; even at this eleventh hour a few were known to be trying to reach the North Atlantic shipping lanes in one last-gasp attempt to regain the initiative!

Fortunately for the Allies, new equipment introduced into Coastal Command service was helping to reverse this temporary ascendancy of the U-boats. ASV radar in the 3cm waveband was far better at detecting periscopes and schnorkel snouts. The American-built Mk VIII and X sets that had entered operational service in the autumn of 1944 were highly regarded but functioned at their best only at short range and in favourable sea conditions. Passive sonar detectors — sonobuoys — were also in use. Dropped in patterns from an aircraft, they were normally used to track a submerged boat after it had been spotted visually or by radar, the signal strength from each buoy being analysed to produce a fix. This equipment, codenamed 'High Tea', was in service with 10 Coastal Command squadrons at the beginning of 1945.

For many months Coastal Command and the Royal Navy had been bracing themselves to deal with a new generation of U-boats, the first of which were known to be preparing for operational deployment. These were the so-called 'electroboats', incorporating the latest advances in technology to increase both their performance and survivability. The most important was the ocean-going Type XXI, possessing three times the battery power of the Type VII, giving it a vastly improved underwater speed (17 knots) and range. Such a vessel could outrun all but the fastest escort ships. The smaller Type XXIII boat was intended for shallow water and coastal operations. The Germans planned to build 381 Type XXIs and 95 Type XXIIIs by May 1945, these to be mass-produced using prefabricated sections built inland and transported by canal to the north German ports for final assembly.

The threat posed by these powerful new U-boats was causing consternation within the Admiralty and further up in the Allied High Command. Bomber Command and the American bomber forces were directed to launch raids against shipyards identified with their assembly, and the U-boat training grounds in the Baltic were sown with hundreds of mines. In February and March Coastal Command contributed by despatching Liberators and Halifaxes from No 18 Group on a succession of night interdiction sorties over the Baltic, where the electroboats were working up.

Fortunately for the Allies, the prospect of having to fight packs of advanced U-boats in a new Atlantic convoy campaign never

Above: The big freeze. Nearly all the aircraft on strength with three Coastal Command squadrons are visible here, drawn up out of the water at Castle Archdale in Northern Ireland as Loch Erne froze over in January 1945. Boats were used to keep parts of the loch free of ice during one of the hardest winters on record. More than 30 aircraft can be seen, including Sunderlands of Nos 201 and 423 RCAF Squadrons and No 202 Squadron's Catalinas.
CH 14837

materialised. Ultimately the bombing raids, transport disruption and production difficulties meant that fewer than half of the planned boats were actually commissioned, and only a handful of these were ready for combat. *U-2324* embarked on the first Type XXIII war patrol on 29 January 1945, and on 25 February *U-2322* sank a merchant ship in the Firth of Forth. Six Type XXIIIs were operational before the end of hostilities, and they torpedoed only four ships. The first and only operational Type XXI was *U-2511*, which finally sailed from Bergen on 30 April, the day Adolf Hitler committed suicide in his Berlin bunker. For all their technological superiority, the electroboats were much too late to have any impact on the war at sea.

Another, altogether more extreme underwater threat to Allied shipping came from midget submarines and 'manned torpedoes'. These had first been used off the invasion coast in the summer of 1944. They were now employed in last-ditch attacks off the Belgian and Dutch coasts, their main target being the supply convoys bound for the Scheldt estuary and Antwerp, but some also attempted to penetrate British coastal waters. The principal types involved were the long-range, two-seat *Seehund* and the short-range, one-manned *Biber* and *Molch* craft. All were armed with two underslung torpedoes. Dealing with these fell to No 16 Group, especially the Albacores and Swordfish of No 119

Squadron and those of the various Fleet Air Arm squadrons attached to Coastal Command. Seven midgets were sunk by Coastal Command aircraft in March. The North Coates Wing was also involved, as was a squadron of Barracudas transferred from the Royal Navy in April. Despite all their efforts the midget submarines were a disaster for the Germans. Between January and April 1945 they sank only 15 small ships, in the process losing many of their number. Some were destroyed in action, but most either foundered at sea or were lost in accidents.

In the anti-shipping war No 248 Squadron withdrew its Mosquito XVIII 'Tsetses' from service in January 1945, as their heavy gun armament was no longer required. The rocket projectile was now the weapon of choice for the Scottish-based strike wings as they continued their rampage along the Norwegian coast. Operations were as hazardous as ever — flak was still the main killer, but the Luftwaffe could be just as deadly. On 15 January the Banff Wing attempted to destroy the already damaged cargo vessel *Claus Rickmers* sheltering in the small port of Leirvik. Five Mosquitos were shot down by the strengthened shore defences or in furious dogfights with FW190s from JG 5. Then, on 9 February, came the infamous 'Black Friday', when nine Beaufighters from the Dallachy Wing were lost to flak and fighters in a disastrous attack on an enemy destroyer in Fordefjord. The losses prompted requests for more Fighter Command Mustangs to be made available for escort duties.

Despite the risks most strike operations met with considerable success. On 17 March three large merchant ships were sunk by the Banff Wing at Alesund, and five more were sunk or set afire at the quayside in Porsgrunn on 30 March. The latter attack was made all the more difficult by the proximity of domestic buildings. Indeed, great pains were taken by the RAF crews on such occasions to avoid civilian casualties, but tragedies were inevitable — and little could be done to protect the Norwegian crews in the ships selected for destruction. In April U-boats became a priority target, as the remnants of Dönitz's command were finally forced out of the Baltic by the Russian advance. The presence of Allied minefields forced many of the fleeing U-boats to surface, and as they made their perilous bids to reach the relative safety of Norway they came within range of the Mosquitos. In a major operation on 9 April the Banff Wing sank three U-boats, although one Mosquito was lost and three others had to put down in Sweden.

With surface vessels now scarce off the Dutch and German coasts, the North Coates Wing had been in action against midget submarines and U-boats, albeit without much success until a *Biber* one-man submarine was sunk on 25 March. No 254 Squadron received a boost to its firepower in April, when four Mosquito XVIII 'Tsetses' were delivered, passed on from No 248 Squadron. Then, on 3 May, with the war almost

over, the Wing enjoyed a last spell of richly deserved success. Two brand-new Type XXI U-boats were caught on the surface, and both were damaged so severely that they were subsequently scuttled by their own crews. On the next day the Beaufighters sank a Type XXIII (*U-2338*) outright and damaged a Type VII, also later scuttled.

No 18 Group's general-reconnaissance squadrons were equally productive in these last days of the war. On 5 May two U-boats were destroyed in the Kattegat by Liberators of Nos 86 and 547 Squadrons, but one Liberator was shot into the sea during the attack. The following day two more U-boats, including a Type XXI, were sunk by No 86 Squadron aircraft. It is perhaps fitting that in these last days of the war the anti-submarine and anti-shipping squadrons should act in concert against a common foe — one that Coastal Command had been battling since the very first day of hostilities and which, more than any other, had come closest to winning the war for Hitler. Coastal Command's final U-boat kill of the war was achieved on 7 May, by a Catalina IV crew of No 210 Squadron operating from Sullom Voe. On 9 May Dönitz ordered his remaining U-boats to surface, fly a black flag of surrender and proceed to Allied ports. Coastal Command's patrols continued until all were accounted for, and the last convoy escort was completed on the night of 3/4 June, by a No 201 Squadron Sunderland.

Below and Right: Halifax crews of No 58 Squadron at Stornoway in the Outer Hebrides, 22-26 February 1945. Coastal Command's other Halifax squadron, No 502, also flew from here. Both units operated against U-boats and shipping off the Norwegian coast, usually by night. In the last months of the war vessels in the Kattegat and Skaggerak became priority targets as the Germans started withdrawing units from Norway and the Baltic ports. The aircraft in the photographs are Merlin-engined Halifax II Series IAs, but these were gradually being replaced by the more effective Hercules-powered Mk IIIs.
CH 14814, CH 14815

Above left: Swordfish IIIs of No 119 Squadron at Knokke le Zout on the Belgian coast, March 1945. Re-formed in the summer of 1944 and initially equipped with No 415 Squadron's Fairey Albacores, the unit flew night anti-shipping patrols off the enemy coast, achieving some successes against U-boats and E-boats. In January 1945 the squadron re-equipped with the Swordfish, fitted with ASV Mk XI radar in a radome between the main undercarriage legs. Midget submarines operating from the Netherlands now became its principal target, and two *Bibers* were sunk on 11 March. **CL 2277**

Left: Beaufighters of No 144 Squadron low over the North Sea on their way back to Dallachy after a strike, March 1945. Formerly torpedo specialists, the squadron had recently switched to using rocket projectiles, now that these had proved to be more effective against shipping, especially in the narrow confines of the Norwegian fjords. Targeting priorities for the strike wings had to be changed after 9 February 1945 — 'Black Friday' — when nine Beaufighters were lost to flak and fighters during an attack on a destroyer and its escorts in Fordefjord (No 404 Squadron RCAF lost six aircraft). Henceforth heavily defended naval vessels were to be ignored in favour of merchant ships and U-boats. **HU 90821**

Above: Three US Navy Liberator (PB4Y-1) squadrons (VPB-103, -105 and -110) had been on loan to Coastal Command for over a year and had recently been joined at Dunkeswell by a detachment from VPB-114. Like RAF Liberators, the PB4Y-1s were fitted with retractable belly radomes and carried a Leigh Light under the starboard wing. A distinctive feature of later versions (based on the B-24J) was their spherical ERCO nose turrets. B-7/U operated with VPB-105. **IWM FLM 1678**

Above: On 11 March 1945 a PB4Y-1 from VPB-103 successfully depth-charged *U-681* west of the Isles of Scilly. The U-boat had already been damaged after hitting a rock while submerged, and its fate was sealed when it was spotted by the American crew. This photograph was taken from the port waist hatch after eight depth charges had been dropped. The Germans were already abandoning their stricken boat, and most of them survived to be picked up by the Royal Navy. **HU 81397**

Above right: Mosquito supreme. A Banff Wing Mosquito VI photographed on final approach after another anti-shipping sortie, April 1945. The recently introduced double-tiered rocket rails visible here allowed aircraft to carry a pair of 50- or 100-gallon drop tanks outboard of the engine nacelles. The extra range meant that the Scottish-based Mosquitos could now bring their devastating firepower to bear on ships and U-boats in the Kattegat. **HU 81401**

Right: One such long-range operation took place on 5 April 1945, when the Banff Wing flew a round trip of over 1,000 miles into the Kattegat, streaking across Denmark at low level. The Mosquitos discovered a convoy of seven ships evacuating German troops back to the Fatherland. In the ensuing attack a flak ship and a trawler were sunk, but one No 235 Squadron Mosquito struck a mast and spun into the sea, killing its crew. Losses among the embarked German troops were heavy. One Canadian pilot later remarked: 'It was one of the heaviest attacks we've made. There was practically no flak … when we left every ship in the convoy was on fire.' **C 5212**

Above: A Warwick V crew of No 179 Squadron at St Eval, April 1945. From left are Flying Officer R. Crighton RAAF, Flight Lieutenant W. O'Dwyer RAAF, Flying Officer G. Leighton, Flying Officer C. Donnelly RAAF, Sergeant B. Braier, Warrant Officer F. Appleton RAAF and Warrant Officer G. Clarke RAAF. The Squadron's only success with the Warwick had come on 24 February 1945, when *U-927* was sunk in the Channel off Falmouth. **HU 81396**

Right and pages 154 and 155: Mosquito versus U-boat. Three photographs taken from a No 143 Squadron Mosquito ('Z-Zebra') on 19 April 1945, during a strike on U-boats in the Kattegat. An intelligence tip-off received the previous day indicated that a convoy of U-boats, including new Type XXI and Type XXIII 'electroboats', had left Kiel for Norway. The Banff Wing laid on an operation involving 22 Mosquitos and intercepted an M-class minesweeper and four surfaced U-boats in line astern. One U-boat quickly crash-dived, but *U-251*, an elderly Type VII, was sunk, and two electroboats severely damaged. The sequence here shows a Type XXIII submerging through a hail of rocket and cannon fire. **HU 81398, HU 81399, HU 81400**

Top: Turkey shoot. In the late afternoon of 21 April 1945 42 Mosquitoes returning from a fruitless sortie in the Kattegat struck gold when they ran into a formation of Ju88 torpedo-bombers intent on attacking Allied shipping off the east coast of Scotland. As this and the following photograph show, the result was a massacre, with nine of the 18 enemy aircraft being shot down in a matter of minutes. The leader of the strike force, Wing Commander Christopher Foxley-Norris, later reported: 'We were returning from an anti-shipping patrol when we ran into the enemy. Soon the sky appeared to be full of exploding aircraft. The engagement was over so quickly that I did not get a chance to sight one myself, but the rest of the boys got in some good shooting.' **C 5220**

Above: Two torpedoes can be seen slung below this Ju88 from KG26, taking hits from a No 248 Squadron Mosquito on 21 April. The RAF pilots found this rare chance to engage enemy aircraft exhilarating. Flight Lieutenant J. Keohane: 'As soon as we saw the enemy markings we went in to attack. They were right down on the water. I let one "88" have a burst and the starboard engine caught fire. He tried to climb away but just stalled and went flop into the sea.' **C 5217**

Above right: Picturesque Norwegian fjords hitherto untouched by the war became a battleground as the strike wings sought out enemy vessels lurking in them during the last months of hostilities. Three Beaufighters from the Dallachy Wing are seen here attacking enemy vessels sheltering beneath the 3,000ft cliffs of Sognefjord on 23 April 1945. The freighter D/S *Ingerseks* was sunk and a couple of flak ships strafed with cannon fire. Two more merchant vessels were left burning after a similar attack in Fedjefjord on 26 April. **C 5274**

Right: Last kill. The crew of this No 210 Squadron Catalina IVA, JX249/X, led by Flight Lieutenant Ken Murray (front row, centre), were responsible for Coastal Command's last successful U-boat attack of the war. At 04.45hrs on 7 May 1945 they detected the snorkel and periscope of *U-320* northwest of Bergen. Four depth charges were released, followed by a pattern of sonobuoys. For many hours the Catalina tracked the underwater sounds of the badly damaged U-boat, helped by other aircraft that arrived on the scene and dropped more sonobuoys. Escaping further attacks, *U-320* limped slowly back to the Norwegian coast, where it was eventually scuttled. **C 5355**

Above: Coastal Command aircraft off the coast of Northern Ireland during operations to escort the last U-boats into captivity in Allied ports, 14 May 1945. In the foreground is Wellington XIV NB814 of No 36 Squadron, with a No 201 Squadron Sunderland in the background. No 36 Squadron had spent most of the war overseas, returning to the UK in 1944, and was based at Benbecula from March 1945. On 4 May 1945 an order to end hostilities had been issued by Admiral Dönitz to the 62 U-boats still at sea. In all, 154 U-boats were captured by the Allies at the end of the war, but the Germans scuttled 227 others, mostly in the western Baltic. **MH 30757**

Above right: Last patrol. The war may have been over, but until all the U-boats at sea had been accounted for Allied shipping had to be protected, and convoy escorts continued in the weeks following the end of hostilities. Finally, in the late afternoon of 3 June 1945, Wing Commander J. Barrett and crew of No 201 Squadron set off from Castle Archdale in Sunderland V 'Z-Zebra' on Coastal Command's last convoy patrol. An official photographer recorded the event. Here the 14-man crew board their aircraft. Barrett was a fitting choice of skipper — he had served throughout the war and had captained one of the Sunderlands involved in the rescue of the crew of the *Kensington Court* in 1939. **CH 15350**

Right: An airwoman chalks up details of Coastal Command's last patrol on the operations board at Castle Archdale. 'Z-Zebra' was sent out into the Atlantic to rendezvous with convoy HX358 some 500 miles southwest of Ireland, making contact at 21.30hrs on 3 June. Just after midnight on 4 June her wireless operator received the signal to return to base. The photographer later wrote: 'With a parting "good sailing, calm seas", Coastal Command's vigilance and watch over Allied shipping in all the sea-lane approaches to the United Kingdom came to an end.' Interesting details are revealed in this shot, including the 'High Tea' reference in the top-left corner of the board, used to identify aircraft fitted with sonobuoy equipment. The war may have been over, but this photograph was considered too sensitive by Air Ministry censors and was duly stopped! **CH 18021**

SELECT BIBLIOGRAPHY

Ashworth, Chris, *RAF Coastal Command 1936-1968* (Patrick Stephens, 1995)

Bowyer, Chaz, *Coastal Command at War* (Ian Allan, 1979)

Bowyer, Chaz, *Men of Coastal Command 1939-45* (William Kimber, 1985)

Buckley, John, *The RAF and Trade Defence 1919-45: Constant Endeavour* (Keele University Press, 1995)

Franks, Norman L. R., *Conflict over the Bay* (William Kimber, 1986)

Franks, Norman L. R., *Search, Find and Kill: Coastal Command's U-boat successes* (Grub Street, 1995)

Goss, Christopher H, *Bloody Biscay: the story of the Luftwaffe's only long-range maritime fighter unit V/KG40 and its adversaries 1942-1944* (Crécy, 1997)

Goulter, Christina J. M., *Forgotten Offensive: Royal Air Force Coastal Command's anti-shipping campaign 1940-45* (Frank Cass, 1995)

Joubert de la Ferté, Sir Philip, *Birds and Fishes — The Story of Coastal Command* (Hutchinson, 1960)

McNeill, Ross, *Royal Air Force Coastal Command Losses of the Second World War 1939-41* (Midland Publishing, 2003)

Nesbit, Roy Conyers, *The Strike Wings: special anti-shipping squadrons 1942-45* (HMSO, 1995)

Rawlings, John D. R., *Coastal, Support and Special Squadrons of the RAF and their Aircraft* (Jane's, 1982)

Terraine, John, *The Right of the Line — The Royal Air Force in the European War 1939-45* (Hodder & Stoughton, 1985)

Sunderland 'Z/Zebra' of No 210 Squadron flies Coastal Command's last operational convoy patrol, 3 June 1945. **CH 15303**